CONDOMINIUM

FINANCING FUNDAMENTALS

A Comprehensive Guide For Real Estate Agents

2023 Edition

Samuel M. Chazanow, CMB

To Toby Harris,

This book is dedicated to you, a visionary, humanitarian, mentor, and co-founder of Movement Mortgage. Your faith, confidence, and trust in me have been the foundation of our incredible journey together.

Your unwavering support has enabled me to build what has been hailed as the best condo approval team in the country. Together, we have achieved remarkable milestones, approving tens of thousands of condominium projects for both conventional and government financing.

Your exceptional leadership and innovative thinking have set a standard of excellence in the industry. Your guidance and wisdom have shaped my understanding of the complex world of condominium financing and empowered me to make a positive impact in the lives of countless individuals and families.

I am grateful for the invaluable lessons you have taught me, the opportunities you have provided, and the unwavering belief you have shown in my abilities. Your mentorship has been instrumental in my professional growth and success.

This dedication is a token of my appreciation for your unwavering support, vision, and commitment to excellence. Your impact on my life and the lives of those we have served together is immeasurable.

Thank you, Toby Harris, for being a guiding light, an inspiration, and a true leader. This book is a tribute to your extraordinary contributions and a testament to the lasting legacy you have created.

With deep respect and gratitude,

Samuel Chazanow, CMB

Contents

Introduction

In the ever-evolving landscape of real estate, condominiums have emerged as a popular choice for home buyers seeking affordability, convenience, amenities, and a vibrant community lifestyle. However, navigating the complex world of condominium financing can be a daunting task for both buyers and real estate agents alike. That's where this book, "Condominium Financing Fundamentals," comes in.

Authored by Samuel Chazanow, a seasoned expert in real estate financing with over 35 years of Mortgage Banking experience, this comprehensive guide is designed to equip real estate agents with the knowledge and tools they need to confidently navigate the intricacies of condominium financing in the United States. With his expertise and industry recognition, Chazanow has become a sought-after speaker and educator, sharing his invaluable insights with thousands of real estate agents nationwide.

As a recipient of the prestigious Certified Mortgage Banker designation by the Mortgage Bankers Association, the highest professional designation in the mortgage banking industry, Chazanow brings a wealth of knowledge and expertise to this book. His passion for helping real estate agents understand the nuances of condominium financing shines through in these pages, making it an indispensable resource for anyone involved in the real estate industry.

"Condominium Financing Fundamentals" delves into the key concepts, strategies, and best practices involved in securing financing for condominiums, covering a wide range of topics such as loan options, underwriting guidelines, legal considerations, market trends, and more. This book offers a comprehensive yet accessible approach to understanding the intricacies of financing condominiums including Fannie Mae and Freddie Mac's recent guideline changes concerning Building Safety, Soundness, Structural Integrity, Habitability and Special Assessments.

Whether you're a seasoned real estate agent looking to expand your expertise or a newcomer to the field seeking a solid foundation in condominium financing, this book will serve as your trusted companion. Its clear and concise explanations, combined with Samuel Chazanow's vast industry experience, will empower you to confidently guide your clients through the complex world of condominium financing, ensuring their success in the competitive real estate market.

Get ready to unlock the secrets of successful condominium financing and elevate your career to new heights with " Condominium Financing Fundamentals: A Comprehensive Guide for Real Estate Agents." Let Samuel Chazanow be your trusted mentor on this exciting journey, as he imparts his wisdom gained from decades of experience, enabling you to navigate the ever-changing landscape of condominium financing with confidence and expertise.

Chapter 1

Understanding Condominiums

1.1 What is a Condominium

As a real estate agent, it is essential to have a clear understanding of what a condominium is, as it is a unique form of property ownership that plays a significant role in the real estate market. A condominium, often referred to as a condo, is a specific type of housing unit that combines individual ownership of a private dwelling unit's "airspace" with shared ownership and responsibility for common areas and amenities within a larger building or complex.

In simpler terms, a condominium is a residential unit that is part of a larger property development or building. Each individual unit owner has exclusive ownership rights to their specific unit, which typically includes the interior space of the unit and sometimes a designated parking spot or storage area. However, beyond their individual units, owners also share ownership and responsibility for common areas such as hallways, lobbies, elevators, recreational facilities, and other amenities provided by the condominium association.

Condominiums are governed by a homeowners association or condominium association, which is responsible for managing and maintaining the common areas and amenities. The association is funded through monthly fees paid by the individual unit owners, often referred to as condominium fees or maintenance fees. These fees contribute to the upkeep of the property, covering expenses such as maintenance, repairs, insurance, landscaping, and other shared services.

Living in a condominium offers several advantages. Condominiums often provide desirable amenities like swimming pools, fitness centers, clubhouses, and 24-hour security. They can also offer a sense of community, as residents share common spaces and often have opportunities for social interaction and organized events. Additionally, condominium living can be appealing for those seeking a more maintenance-free lifestyle, as the association takes care of many exterior maintenance tasks.

It's important for real estate agents to be familiar with the legal and financial aspects of condominium ownership. Prospective buyers should be informed about the governing documents, such as the declaration, bylaws, and rules and regulations of the condominium association. These documents outline the rights, responsibilities, and restrictions that come with owning a condominium unit.

Understanding the intricacies of condominium ownership, including the financing options, legal considerations, and the roles and responsibilities of the association, will enable real estate agents to effectively assist their clients in navigating the complexities of condominium transactions and guide them towards making informed decisions when buying or selling condominium properties.

1.2 Types of Condominiums

Real estate agents play a crucial role in guiding clients through the diverse range of condominium options available in urban, suburban, rural and resort markets. It's important to have a clear understanding of the different types of condominiums to effectively match clients' needs and preferences with the right property. Here are some common types of condominiums found in these markets:

High-Rise Condominiums:

- High-rise condominiums are typically found in urban areas and feature tall buildings with multiple floors.

- These condominiums often offer spectacular views of the city skyline or nearby natural attractions.

- Amenities can include concierge services, fitness centers, rooftop terraces, and communal areas.

Low-Rise Condominiums:

- Low-rise condominiums are usually smaller-scale buildings with fewer floors, typically found in suburban areas.

- They often feature a more intimate community atmosphere and may have landscaped grounds or outdoor spaces.

- Amenities can include swimming pools, outdoor recreation areas, and shared facilities like party rooms or gyms.

Townhouse Condominiums:

- Townhouse condominiums are multi-level units that share one or two walls with neighboring units.

- These properties often resemble traditional townhouses and offer a combination of privacy and shared amenities.

- They can be found in both urban and suburban areas, providing a balance between single-family homes and apartment-style living.

Mixed-Use Condominiums:

- Mixed-use condominiums combine residential units with commercial or retail spaces in the same building or development.

- These condominiums are common in urban areas and provide a blend of residential convenience and access to nearby amenities and services.

- Residents may have easy access to shops, restaurants, offices, or entertainment venues within the same complex.

Resort Condominiums:

- Resort condominiums are typically located in vacation destinations or areas with scenic beauty, such as beachfront or mountainous regions.

- These condominiums cater to seasonal or vacation-oriented living and often offer resort-style amenities like pools, spas, golf courses, and beach access.

- Resort condominiums may have rental programs, allowing owners to generate income from their units when not in use.

Luxury Condominiums:

- Luxury condominiums are high-end properties that offer premium features, finishes, and amenities.

- They are often located in prime urban or resort areas and provide a luxurious living experience.

- Amenities can include private elevators, 24/7 security,

top-of-the-line appliances, premium materials, and exclusive access to facilities like private clubs or spas.

Single-family Detached Condos:

Detached condos, know as "site condos", are a hybrid between traditional detached housing and condominiums. Detached condos can either be built on the lot or manufactured in a factory and delivered to the lot. Like traditional detached houses, detached condos offer individual ownership of the dwelling and the land it sits on. Each unit is owned separately, giving the homeowners a sense of control and responsibility over their property. Despite being individual units, detached condos often come with shared community amenities which are typically maintained and managed by the Homeowners Association (HOA) and funded by monthly dues paid by the unit owners. One of the significant benefits of detached condos is that the exterior maintenance and landscaping are usually taken care of by the HOA.

Understanding the various types of condominiums in urban, suburban, rural, and resort markets enables real estate agents to match their clients' preferences, lifestyles, and investment goals with the right property. By having in-depth knowledge of these options, agents can provide valuable guidance and help clients make informed decisions in their condominium purchase or sale transactions.

1.3 Advantages and Disadvantages of Condominium Ownership

As a real estate agent, it is crucial to understand the advantages and disadvantages of different types of ownership structures to effectively guide clients in their property decisions. Here is a comparison of condominium ownership to Planned Unit Developments (PUD),

Cooperatives (Co-ops), and Single-family homes:

Condominium Ownership: Advantages:

Affordability: Condominiums often provide a more affordable option compared to single-family homes, especially in urban areas with high property prices.

Amenities and Services: Condominiums frequently offer shared amenities such as pools, fitness centers, and maintenance services, providing convenience and additional lifestyle benefits.

Limited Maintenance Responsibility: Condominium owners typically have limited maintenance responsibilities as the association handles common area upkeep and exterior maintenance.

Shared Decision-Making: Owners have a voice in the management and decision-making process of the condominium association through elected boards or committees.

Disadvantages:

Homeowners Association (HOA) Fees: Condominium owners are obligated to pay monthly HOA fees, which cover shared expenses, but can add to the overall cost of ownership.

Limited Privacy and Control: Condominium owners must adhere to association rules and regulations, limiting their ability to modify or personalize their units and sometimes imposing restrictions on rental or pet policies.

Potential for Special Assessments: Owners may face unexpected expenses if the association imposes special assessments to cover significant repairs or improvements.

Planned Unit Developments (PUD): Advantages:

More Freedom and Control: PUD owners typically have more flexibility in modifying their homes and landscaping compared to condominium owners.

Access to Amenities: PUD often include amenities like parks, playgrounds, and common areas that enhance the community's appeal.

Potential for Yard and Outdoor Space: PUD often provide individual yards or outdoor areas, which can be desirable for homeowners seeking more private outdoor space

Disadvantages:

Greater Maintenance Responsibility: PUD owners are responsible for maintaining their individual units and outdoor spaces, which can involve additional costs and efforts.

Potential for HOA Regulations: Some PUDs have homeowners associations that enforce rules and architectural guidelines to maintain the community's appearance and value.

Homeowners Association Fees: PUD owners may be subject to HOA fees to cover shared amenities and maintenance of common areas.

Cooperatives (Co-ops): Advantages:

Shared Expenses: Co-op owners share expenses, including

property taxes, maintenance, and utilities, which can result in lower individual costs compared to single-family homes.

Potential for Affordability: Co-op units are often more affordable compared to condominiums or single-family homes in the same area.

Community and Security: Co-ops can provide a sense of community and security as residents collectively govern and look out for one another.

Disadvantages:

Limited Control: Co-op owners have limited control over their units and must abide by strict rules and regulations set by the cooperative board.

Difficult Financing: Financing a co-op purchase can be more challenging compared to condominiums or single-family homes, as lenders often have specific requirements since the collateral is not real estate, its actually shares of stock of the co-op corporation.

Potential for Co-op Board Approval: Prospective buyers must go through a rigorous application process and obtain approval from the co-op board, which can be time-consuming and restrictive.

Single-Family Homes: Advantages:

Privacy and Control: Single-family homeowners have greater control over their property, allowing for customization, renovations, and landscaping according to their preferences.

Independence: Homeowners are not subject to the rules and regulations of an association and have more freedom to make decisions regarding their property.

Potential for Investment and Appreciation: Single-family homes often have greater potential for long-term appreciation and can serve as an investment.

Disadvantages:

Higher Maintenance Responsibility: Single-family homeowners bear the full responsibility for property maintenance, repairs, and landscaping.

Higher Costs: Single-family homes typically have higher upfront costs and ongoing expenses compared to condominiums or cooperatives.

Limited Shared Amenities: Unlike condominiums or cooperatives, single-family homeowners may not have access to shared amenities like pools, fitness centers, or community spaces.

By understanding the advantages and disadvantages of different ownership structures, real estate agents can effectively guide their clients in making informed decisions based on their preferences, financial circumstances, and lifestyle needs.

1.4 The Role of Real Estate Agents in Condominium Transactions

Real estate agents play a crucial role in facilitating successful condominium transactions. Their expertise, knowledge, and guidance are invaluable to both buyers and sellers throughout the process. Here are some key aspects of the real estate agent's role in condominium transactions:

Educating Buyers and Sellers: Real estate agents provide essential information to buyers and sellers about condominiums. They explain the unique aspects of condominium ownership, including shared responsibilities, association fees, and restrictions imposed by the condominium association. Agents educate clients on the benefits and considerations of owning a condominium and help them make informed decisions based on their specific needs and preferences.

Identifying Suitable Properties: Real estate agents help buyers find condominiums that meet their criteria. They use their knowledge of the local market, understanding of the client's preferences, and access to listing databases to identify properties that match the client's desired location, size, amenities, and budget. Agents can also provide insights into upcoming or off-market opportunities.

Marketing and Listing Condominiums: When representing sellers, real estate agents create effective marketing strategies to promote the condominiums and attract potential buyers. They leverage various marketing channels, such as online listings, professional photography, virtual tours, and open houses, to showcase the unique features and advantages of the property. Agents also utilize their networks and connections to reach out to potential buyers and other agents who may have interested clients.

Negotiating and Structuring Deals: Real estate agents play an essential role in negotiating and structuring deals between buyers and sellers. They facilitate communication between parties, helping to bridge any gaps in expectations or preferences. Agents use their negotiation skills to advocate for their clients' best interests, whether it involves price negotiations, contingencies, repairs, or other aspects of the transaction. They also help draft and review purchase agreements, ensuring that all necessary details and contingencies are included.

Coordinating Professionals and Resources: Real estate agents collaborate with other professionals involved in the condominium transaction process. They coordinate with mortgage lenders and brokers, home inspectors, appraisers, title companies, and attorneys to ensure a smooth and timely closing. Agents guide their clients through the necessary steps, providing recommendations and resources for reputable professionals, which streamlines the process and instills confidence in their clients.

Providing Market Insights: Real estate agents keep abreast of market trends and developments in the condominium sector. They provide clients with valuable insights on pricing, market conditions, and investment potential. Agents share their knowledge of comparable sales, recent transactions, and market forecasts, enabling clients to make informed decisions and negotiate effectively.

Throughout the entire process, real estate agents act as trusted advisors and advocates for their clients. They navigate the complexities of condominium transactions, providing guidance, expertise, and support from the initial property search to the final closing. By leveraging their knowledge, experience, and network, real estate agents ensure a smooth and successful condominium transaction for their clients and create opportunities for future referrals.

Chapter 2

Condominium Financing Basics

2.1 Overview of Condominium Financing

As a real estate agent, understanding the basics of condominium financing is essential to effectively guide your clients through the process of purchasing or selling a condominium. Here is an overview of condominium financing that will help you assist your clients in navigating this aspect of their transaction:

Mortgage Options: Condominium buyers typically finance their purchase through a mortgage loan. It's important to familiarize yourself with the various mortgage options available to your clients, such as conventional loans, government-backed loans (e.g., FHA, VA, USDA), and specialty financing programs, known as "non-warrantable", specifically designed for condominiums.

Down Payments: Lenders may have varying requirements for down payments on condominiums. This will be discussed in greater detail in Chapter 10. Ensure you are aware of the minimum down payment percentages and any additional guidelines specific to condominium financing, "overlays", your borrower's lender may have. Communicate this information to your clients to help them plan and prepare for the financial aspect of their purchase.

Lender Approval: Lenders will conduct an evaluation of the condominium project to determine its eligibility for financing.

This process, known as a condominium project approval or review, assesses factors such as the financial stability of the condominium association, project risk characteristics, master insurance to indemnify the HOA in the event of property damage or liability claims, and the condition of the property. Understanding the lender approval process will enable you to identify potential financing challenges early on and guide your clients accordingly.

Condominium Association Documents: Familiarize yourself with the key documents that govern the condominium association, such as the declaration, bylaws, and rules and regulations. These documents contain important information that lenders will review during the financing process. Work closely with your clients and their lenders to ensure that all necessary documentation is obtained and provided in a timely manner.

Condominium Fees and Assessments: Condominium buyers will have ongoing financial obligations in the form of condominium fees, also known as maintenance fees or HOA fees. These fees cover the costs associated with maintaining and managing the common areas and amenities. It's crucial to help your clients understand the financial implications of these fees and factor them into their budgeting and affordability calculations.

Additional Considerations: Advise your clients on potential financing challenges they may encounter in certain situations, such as non-warrantable condominiums, condominium conversions, or new construction projects. These scenarios may require specialized financing options or additional due diligence.

Collaborating with Lenders: Establish relationships with lenders who specialize in condominium financing or have experience working with condominium projects. Collaborating closely with lenders can help streamline the financing process and ensure that your clients receive the necessary guidance and support.

By having a solid understanding of condominium financing, you can effectively communicate with your clients, anticipate potential challenges, and guide them through the intricacies of securing financing for their condominium purchase or sale. Stay informed about changes in lending guidelines and industry trends to provide the most up-to-date information and advice to your clients.

2.2 Key Differences Between Conventional Home Loans and Condominium Loans

Real estate agents need to understand the key differences between conventional home loans and condominium loans to effectively guide their clients through the financing process. Here are the main distinctions between these two types of loans:

Property Eligibility: One of the primary differences lies in the property eligibility criteria. Lenders often have specific requirements for each loan type. With conventional home loans, lenders focus on factors such as the borrower's creditworthiness, income stability, employment history, debt-to-income ratio and collateral condition and value. In addition, condominium loans have additional requirements that pertain specifically to the condominium project. Lenders evaluate the financial health of the condominium association, project risk factors, insurance coverage of the project, the condition and marketability of the project.

Condominium Association Approval: For condominium loans, lenders typically require the condominium project to be approved by the lender or meet certain eligibility criteria. This means that the project itself must meet specific guidelines established by the lender to ensure the project's financial stability and compliance with lending standards. This approval process is not required for conventional home loans for single family homes, 2-4 family homes or homes located in a Planned Unit Developments (PUD).

Down Payment and Mortgage Insurance: The down payment requirements of conventional home loans and condominium loans are the same according to current Fannie Mae and Freddie Mac guidelines. However, HOA legal documents can mandate minimum down payment requirements greater than Fannie Mae and Freddie Mac guidelines and lenders may have "overlays" requiring larger down payments due to perceived risks associated with condominium financing.

Appraisal Considerations: The appraisal process for condominium loans may have additional requirements. Appraisers may need to assess the value of the individual condominium unit as well as the overall financial health, condition and marketability of the entire condominium project. This helps determine whether the property meets the lender's guidelines and supports the loan amount.

It is important for real estate agents to be aware of these key differences between conventional home loans and condominium loans. This understanding allows agents to provide accurate and relevant information to their clients, effectively communicate with lenders, and help their clients navigate the specific requirements and considerations of securing financing for a condominium purchase.

2.3 Financing Options for Condominium Buyers

Real estate agents should have a comprehensive understanding of the various financing options available to condominium buyers. Here's an overview of the three main categories of financing options:

Traditional Mortgage Financing: Traditional mortgage financing, also known as conventional loans, is a popular option for condominium buyers. These loans are typically offered by banks, credit unions, and mortgage lenders. Key features of traditional mortgage financing include:

Down Payment: Conventional loans often require a down payment ranging from 3% to 20% of the purchase price, depending on the borrower's creditworthiness and the lender's requirements.

Private Mortgage Insurance (PMI): If the down payment is less than 20%, borrowers may need to pay for PMI, which protects the lender in case of default. PMI can be canceled once the borrower's equity reaches a certain threshold.

Interest Rates: Conventional loans offer competitive interest rates based on the borrower's credit score, loan amount, and other factors.

Loan Terms: Conventional loans typically come with various loan term options, such as 15-year or 30-year fixed-rate mortgages or adjustable-rate mortgages (ARMs).

Lender Requirements: Borrowers need to meet specific credit score, income, asset, and debt-to-income ratio requirements set by the lender.

Government-backed loan programs provide additional options for condominium buyers who may face challenges with traditional financing. It is essential for real estate agents to be familiar with these programs to assist their clients effectively. Here's an overview of the three main government-backed loan programs for condominium financing:

Federal Housing Administration (FHA) Loans: FHA loans are insured by the Federal Housing Administration and are widely used for condominium financing. Key features of FHA loans include:

- Lower Down Payment: FHA loans offer a low down payment option, typically as low as 3.5% of the purchase price. This makes it more accessible for buyers who have limited funds for a down payment.

- Flexible Qualification Criteria: FHA loans have more lenient credit score requirements and may consider borrowers with a lower credit score. This can be advantageous for buyers who have less established credit or a lower credit score.

- Condominium Project Guidelines: FHA loans have specific guidelines for condominium projects that must be met, such as a certain percentage of owner-occupied units, minimum rental period, and financial stability of the condominium association.

Veterans Affairs (VA) Loans: VA loans are available to eligible veterans, active-duty service members, and their spouses. Key features of VA loans include:

No Down Payment: VA loans offer 100% financing, meaning no down payment is required for qualified borrowers. This can be a significant benefit for eligible veterans and active-duty service members.

Competitive Interest Rates: VA loans generally have competitive interest rates, which can save borrowers money over the life of the loan.

Condominium Project Eligibility: VA loans have specific requirements for condominium projects, including being approved by the VA and meeting certain criteria to ensure the project's compliance with VA guidelines.

United States Department of Agriculture (USDA) Loans: USDA loans are specifically designed for home buyers in rural and suburban areas. Key features of USDA loans include:

No Down Payment: USDA loans offer 100% financing, eliminating the need for a down payment.

Affordable Housing: USDA loans aim to promote affordable home ownership in eligible rural areas, making them an attractive option for buyers looking to purchase in those locations.

Income and Property Eligibility: USDA loans have income and property eligibility requirements, including the location of the property in an eligible rural area and meeting certain income limits.

Portfolio Loans: Portfolio loans are held by individual lenders instead of being sold to secondary markets. These loans may offer more flexibility in underwriting criteria, allowing for non-traditional sources of income or unique property types.

Non-Qualified Mortgage (Non-QM) Loans: Non-QM loans are designed for borrowers who do not meet traditional qualification standards. These loans consider alternative factors such as asset-based income, bank statements, or other unconventional income sources.

Seller Financing: In some cases, the seller may offer financing options to the buyer, often referred to as seller financing or owner financing. This arrangement involves the seller acting as the lender and allowing the buyer to make payments directly to them over a specified period.

Real estate agents should stay informed about the availability, requirements, and limitations of these financing options. By understanding the various financing possibilities, agents can assist their clients in selecting the most suitable option for their specific circumstances and help them navigate the intricacies of the financing process in condominium transactions.

2.4 The Role of Lenders in Condominium Financing

Lenders play a crucial role in condominium financing, as they provide the funds that enable buyers to purchase condominium units. Here's an explanation of the key role of lenders in condominium financing:

Loan Origination: Lenders originate loans by working directly with borrowers to evaluate their eligibility, assess their financial situation, and determine the loan amount for which they qualify. In the case of condominium financing, lenders review specific factors related to the property and the borrower's qualifications to ensure compliance with their lending standards.

Pre-Approval Process: Lenders offer pre-approval services to prospective condominium buyers. During the pre-approval process, lenders review the borrower's financial documents, such as income verification, credit history, and assets, to determine their borrowing capacity and provide them with a pre-approval letter. This letter demonstrates the buyer's ability to secure financing, which strengthens their position when making an offer on a condominium.

Condominium Project Evaluation: In condominium financing, lenders assess the eligibility of the condominium project itself. They review factors such as the financial stability of the condominium association, condition of the project and other project risk factors such as pending litigation or other issues that may affect the project's viability. Lenders must ensure that the project meets their guidelines and lending standards before approving financing for individual units within the project.

Down Payment and Loan-to-Value Ratio: Lenders establish the down payment requirements for condominium financing based on agency guidelines and internal "overlay" policy. The down payment is the initial upfront payment made by the buyer towards the purchase price of the condominium. Lenders also determine the loan-to-value (LTV) ratio, which represents the percentage of the purchase price that can be financed through the loan. The down payment and LTV ratio are critical factors that affect the borrower's financing options and the overall terms of the loan.

Mortgage Underwriting: Lenders conduct the mortgage underwriting process to assess the borrower's financial risk and determine if they qualify for a loan. Underwriting involves reviewing the borrower's creditworthiness, income, debt-to-income ratio, employment history, and other relevant factors. For condominium financing, lenders may also review the financial health and condition of the condominium association and evaluate the borrower's ability to meet the condominium fees and assessments.

Loan Terms and Interest Rates: Lenders offer various loan terms and interest rate options to borrowers. The loan term refers to the length of time over which the borrower will repay the loan, such as 15, 20, or 30 years. The interest rate represents the cost of borrowing and is influenced by market conditions, the borrower's creditworthiness, and the overall risk associated with the loan. Lenders provide borrowers with loan options and guide them in selecting the most suitable terms and interest rates for their condominium financing.

Loan Servicing: After the loan is closed, lenders may choose to service the loan themselves or transfer the servicing rights to another company. Loan servicing involves collecting monthly payments from borrowers, managing escrow accounts (if applicable), providing customer support, and ensuring compliance with loan terms and requirements. Borrowers communicate with the loan servicer for any inquiries or concerns related to their loan.

Real estate agents should work closely with lenders to help their clients navigate the financing process, understand the lender's requirements, and facilitate a smooth transaction. Having a strong relationship with lenders who specialize in condominium financing can significantly benefit agents and their clients, ensuring a seamless and successful condominium purchase or sale.

Chapter 3

Government Condominium Loans: Affordable and Assumable

3.1 VA Condominium Loans

The Veterans Administration (VA), now known as the U.S. Department of Veterans Affairs, has a rich history of supporting veterans in various ways, including providing accessible home financing options. One such option is the VA Home Loan program, which plays a vital role in helping eligible veterans, active-duty service members, and surviving spouses achieve homeownership.

A significant advantage of VA loans is that they are often offered with competitive fixed interest rates. This means that veterans can secure a loan with a consistent interest rate throughout the loan term, providing stability and predictability in their monthly mortgage payments. VA no longer has maximum geographic loan limits which is extremely beneficial to eligible veterans who can qualify for higher priced luxury condominiums. Moreover, an important fact about fixed-rate VA loans is their assumable feature. This means that qualified veterans, as well as non-veterans, may have the opportunity to assume or take over the existing VA loan from the original borrower. This feature can be advantageous in certain scenarios, such as when interest rates have increased, allowing the buyer to assume the loan at the original favorable rate.

For real estate agents working with veterans, it's crucial to understand and communicate this valuable aspect of fixed-rate VA loans. By highlighting the assumable feature, you can provide additional options and potential benefits to both veterans and non-veterans who may be interested in purchasing a home through assuming an existing VA loan.

Assisting clients in navigating the VA loan program, explaining the benefits, and facilitating the process of assuming a VA loan can help you better serve your clients and contribute to their successful homeownership journey.

It is important to Stay updated with the latest guidelines and requirements related to assumable VA loans to ensure you can provide accurate information and guidance to your clients. By leveraging the benefits of the VA loan program, you can make a meaningful impact in helping veterans and non-veterans achieve their homeownership dreams.

3.2 FHA Condominium Loans

The Federal Housing Administration (FHA) has played a significant role in promoting homeownership and providing affordable financing options since its establishment in 1934. The FHA is a part of the U.S. Department of Housing and Urban Development (HUD) and operates with a mission to expand homeownership opportunities for low- to moderate-income individuals and families.

One of the FHA's essential programs is the FHA-insured mortgage loan program. FHA loans are designed to provide accessible and affordable financing to homebuyers. These loans are backed by the FHA, reducing the risk for lenders and allowing them to offer favorable terms to borrowers.

FHA loans for condominiums often feature lower down payment requirements, more flexible credit qualifications, and competitive interest rates. These factors make them an attractive option for condo buyers who may have limited funds for a down payment or may not meet the stringent requirements of conventional loans.

Moreover, it's important to note that fixed-rate FHA loans are assumable. This means that qualified borrowers may have the opportunity to assume or take over the existing FHA loan from the original borrower. This can be advantageous for buyers, as it allows them to inherit the favorable terms and interest rate of the original loan, even if market rates have increased.

As a real estate agent, it's vital to be knowledgeable about the FHA loan program and its benefits for condo buyers. Understanding the eligibility requirements, geographic loan limits, and guidelines specific to FHA-insured condominium financing can help you effectively guide your clients through the process.

Highlighting the benefits of FHA loans, including their affordability, flexible credit requirements, and assumable feature, can attract condo buyers and expand your clientele. By staying informed about any updates or changes to the FHA loan program, you can provide accurate information and guide your clients toward suitable financing options.

Helping condo buyers navigate the FHA loan process and maximizing the benefits of FHA financing can make a significant difference in their ability to achieve affordable homeownership.

3.3 USDA Condominium Loans

The U.S. Department of Agriculture (USDA) has played a vital role in supporting rural communities and promoting homeownership through its various programs. One such program is the USDA Single Family Housing Guaranteed Loan Program, which assists low- to moderate-income borrowers in purchasing homes, including eligible condominiums, in rural areas.

The USDA program aims to improve the quality of life in rural areas by making homeownership more attainable and affordable for individuals and families. It provides lenders with a guarantee on loans made to qualified borrowers, which reduces the risk for lenders and allows them to offer favorable terms and low down payment requirements.

USDA loans offer several benefits for homebuyers in rural areas, including competitive fixed interest rates, flexible credit requirements, and no private mortgage insurance (PMI) requirement. These features make them an attractive option for borrowers who may not qualify for traditional financing or who seek affordable homeownership in rural communities.

Additionally, it's important to note that all fixed-rate USDA loans are assumable. Similarly to VA and FHA, qualified buyers have the opportunity to assume an existing USDA loan from the original borrower. This can be advantageous in situations where interest rates have increased, as the buyer can assume the original loan's favorable fixed interest rate, even if market rates have gone up.

For real estate agents operating in rural areas, understanding the USDA loan program and its benefits is crucial. By being knowledgeable about the eligibility requirements, loan limits, and guidelines specific to USDA financing, you can effectively guide your clients through the homebuying process and connect them with lenders experienced in USDA loans.

Highlighting the advantages of USDA loans, including their affordability, low down payment requirements, and assumable feature, can attract prospective buyers and expand your clientele in rural areas. It is important to stay up-to-date with any changes or updates to the USDA loan program to provide accurate and current information to clients.

Assisting homebuyers in navigating the USDA loan process and maximizing the benefits of USDA financing can significantly contribute to their ability to achieve affordable homeownership in rural communities.

Chapter 4

Condominium Association Documents

4.1 Understanding the Declarations and Bylaws

The condominium Declaration and Bylaws are important legal documents that govern the operation and management of a condominium association. Real estate agents should understand the purpose and significance of these documents when assisting clients in condominium transactions. Here's an explanation:

Declaration: The Declaration, also known as the Master Deed or Covenants, Conditions, and Restrictions (CC&R), is a foundational document that establishes the legal framework for the condominium project. Its primary purpose is to outline the rights and responsibilities of the individual unit owners, as well as the obligations and powers of the condominium association. Here's what agents should know about the Declaration:

Unit Boundaries and Common Elements: The Declaration defines the boundaries of each individual condominium unit and designates the shared or common elements of the property, such as hallways, elevators, roofs, and amenities like swimming pools or fitness centers.

Unit Owner Rights and Obligations: The Declaration outlines the rights and obligations of the individual unit owners, including their responsibilities for maintenance, repair, and use of their units, as well as any restrictions on modifications or alterations to the property.

Association Powers and Responsibilities: The Declaration specifies the powers and responsibilities of the condominium association, such as collecting and managing association fees, enforcing rules and regulations, maintaining common areas, and making decisions related to the operation and governance of the condominium project.

Bylaws: The Bylaws are another important document that provides detailed rules and procedures for the operation and management of the condominium association. The Bylaws supplement the Declaration by further defining the association's structure, governance, and decision-making processes. Here's what real estate agents should understand about the Bylaws:

Association Governance: The Bylaws outline the structure and composition of the association's board of directors or trustees, including the election or appointment processes. They may also establish terms of office, voting procedures, and the responsibilities and powers of the board.

Meeting Procedures: The Bylaws define the procedures for conducting association meetings, including regular meetings, annual meetings, and special meetings. They may specify notice requirements, quorum thresholds, and voting procedures for various matters.

Assessment and Fee Collection: The Bylaws outline the process for determining and collecting association fees, commonly referred to as maintenance fees or HOA fees. They may specify the frequency of assessments, the methods of fee calculation, and the consequences for non-payment.

Rule Enforcement: The Bylaws establish the authority of the association to enforce rules and regulations within the condominium project. They define the procedures for addressing violations, issuing warnings or fines, and resolving disputes between unit owners or between owners and the association.

Understanding the Declaration and Bylaws is crucial for real estate agents as these documents outline the rights and obligations of buyers and sellers in a condominium project. Agents should ensure that their clients review and understand these documents before making any commitments to purchase or sell a condominium unit. They should also be prepared to answer questions or direct clients to legal professionals for further clarification or advice regarding the content of the Declaration and Bylaws.

4.2 Reviewing the Master Deed and Plat Map

The Master Deed and Plat Map are essential documents in understanding and conveying the ownership and layout of a condominium project. Real estate agents should grasp the importance of these documents when assisting clients in condominium transactions. Here's an explanation:

Master Deed: The Master Deed, also known as the Condominium Declaration or Condominium Master Declaration, is a legally binding document that establishes the condominium project and defines the rights and responsibilities of unit owners and the condominium association. Here's why the Master Deed is important:

Ownership and Boundaries: The Master Deed provides a detailed description of the individual units and common areas within the condominium project. It outlines the precise boundaries of each unit, including the interior "airspace", as well as any exclusive-use areas or "limited common elements" such as parking spaces, docks or storage units.

Shared Elements and Amenities: The Master Deed specifies the common elements and amenities available to all unit owners within the condominium project. This can include hallways, elevators, recreational areas, and shared utilities. It clarifies the shared ownership and use rights for these elements.

Restrictions and Regulations: The Master Deed establishes the rules and regulations that govern the use, maintenance, and modification of the individual units and common areas. It may outline restrictions on activities, noise levels, pet policies, rentals or architectural modifications. Agents should ensure that buyers are aware of these restrictions and that they align with their clients' preferences

Plat Map: The Plat Map, also known as the Condominium Plan or Site Plan, is a visual representation of the condominium project's layout and boundaries. It is typically prepared by a surveyor and plays a vital role in understanding the spatial arrangement of the units and common areas.

Here's why the Plat Map is important:

Unit Locations and Numbers: The Plat Map displays the location of each individual unit within the condominium project, including their position within the building or complex. It provides a visual reference for buyers to understand the unit's orientation, proximity to amenities, and neighboring units.

Common Area Designation: The Plat Map clearly demarcates the boundaries of the common areas and amenities within the condominium project. It helps buyers visualize the distribution of shared spaces and amenities, such as pools, parking areas, or green spaces.

Easements and Encroachments: The Plat Map may identify easements or encroachments that affect the property. Easements could grant rights of access or utility lines across certain areas, while encroachments may show instances where a unit or structure extends beyond its designated boundaries.

Understanding the Master Deed and Plat Map allows real estate agents to communicate crucial information to their clients. Agents can use these documents to clarify ownership rights, explain the layout of the condominium project, highlight restrictions or amenities, and address any concerns buyers may have. By reviewing and interpreting these documents, agents can ensure that their clients make informed decisions when buying or selling a condominium unit.

4.3 Importance of HOA Rules and Regulations

Real estate agents should understand the importance of Homeowners Association (HOA) Rules and Regulations when assisting clients in purchasing a condominium unit. These rules govern the operation and conduct within the condominium community and can significantly impact a buyer's decision. Here's an explanation of their significance:

Maintaining Community Standards: HOA Rules and Regulations set the standards for acceptable behavior, appearance, and use of the common areas and individual units. They establish guidelines for maintaining the overall aesthetic appeal and quality of life within the condominium community. Examples may include rules regarding noise levels, pet policies, parking restrictions, or architectural modifications.

Protecting Property Values: The HOA Rules and Regulations play a vital role in preserving property values within the condominium community. By enforcing standards and restrictions, they help maintain a cohesive and attractive environment. Consistent adherence to these rules ensures that all residents contribute to maintaining the overall desirability and marketability of the condominium complex.

Shared Responsibility and Cooperation: HOA Rules and Regulations promote a sense of shared responsibility and cooperation among residents. By establishing guidelines for common areas, amenities, and the use of shared facilities, they help foster a harmonious living environment and prevent conflicts among residents. These rules can create a sense of community and contribute to a positive living experience.

Assessing Compliance and Enforcement: The HOA is responsible for enforcing the Rules and Regulations within the condominium community. They have the authority to levy fines or penalties for violations, encourage compliance through warnings or notices, and resolve disputes between residents. It's important for buyers to understand the enforcement procedures and consequences for non-compliance to ensure they can adhere to the established guidelines.

Impact on Lifestyle and Personal Preferences: The HOA Rules and Regulations can significantly impact a buyer's lifestyle and personal preferences. For example, if a buyer has specific preferences regarding pet ownership, parking arrangements, renting or property modifications, they must review the HOA Rules and Regulations to ensure they align with their desired lifestyle. Buyers should carefully assess the rules to determine if they can comfortably comply with them and if the rules are compatible with their lifestyle choices.

Understanding the HOA Rules and Regulations is essential for real estate agents as they guide their clients in making informed decisions. Agents should review these rules with their clients, highlighting any restrictions or guidelines that may impact their lifestyle or personal preferences. By providing a clear understanding of the rules, agents can help buyers evaluate whether the condominium community aligns with their needs, preferences, and future plans, enabling them to make informed decisions when purchasing a unit.

Chapter 5

Mortgage Approval Process for Condominiums

5.1 Preparing Buyers for the Mortgage Approval Process

Preparing buyers for the mortgage approval process is an important role for real estate agents. By providing guidance and assistance, agents can help buyers navigate the process more smoothly. Here are key steps to prepare buyers for the mortgage approval process:

Early Education: Start by educating buyers about the mortgage approval process early in their home buying journey. Explain the importance of credit scores, debt-to-income ratios, and other key factors that lenders consider when evaluating loan applications. Encourage buyers to review their credit reports and address any inaccuracies or negative items.

Connect with Lenders: Help buyers connect with reputable lenders who offer competitive rates and have experience in the local market. Encourage buyers to reach out to lenders early on to get pre-qualified or pre-approved for a mortgage. This process helps buyers understand their budget, strengthens their position when making offers, and expedites the loan application once they find a property.

Gather Documentation: Advise buyers on the documents required for the mortgage application. This typically includes income verification (pay stubs, tax returns, W-2s), asset statements (bank statements, investment accounts), identification documents, and other relevant paperwork. Encourage buyers to gather these documents in advance to avoid delays during the approval process.

Budget Planning: Help buyers create a realistic budget that considers not only the mortgage payment but also other homeownership expenses such as property taxes, insurance, and maintenance costs. Discuss the potential impact of different loan terms, interest rates, and down payment options on their monthly payments and long-term financial commitments.

Maintain Financial Stability: Remind buyers to maintain financial stability throughout the homebuying process. Discourage major purchases or opening new credit accounts during this time, as it could impact their creditworthiness and affect the mortgage approval. Encourage responsible financial behavior and prompt bill payments to maintain a favorable financial profile.

Review Loan Options: Review different loan options with buyers, including down payment assistance programs, government-backed loans, or specialty loan programs that cater to specific needs or circumstances. Help buyers understand the pros and cons of each option and how they align with their financial situation and homeownership goals.

Communicate and Coordinate: Foster open communication between buyers, lenders, and other professionals involved in the transaction. Encourage buyers to promptly respond to requests from the lender and provide any additional documentation or information as needed. Coordinate with the lender, escrow officer, and other parties to ensure a smooth and timely mortgage approval process.

By guiding buyers through these steps, real estate agents can help prepare them for the mortgage approval process. Clear communication, education, and proactive planning will empower buyers to navigate the process more confidently, increasing the chances of a successful mortgage approval and ultimately securing their desired property.

5.2 Assessing the Condominium Project's Eligibility

Real estate agents should understand the factors lenders consider when determining the eligibility of a condominium project for financing through entities such as Fannie Mae (FNMA), Freddie Mac (FHLMC), the Department of Veterans Affairs (VA), the Federal Housing Administration (FHA), or the United States Department of Agriculture (USDA). Here's an explanation of the key criteria:

FNMA and FHLMC Eligibility: To determine if a condominium project meets FNMA or FHLMC eligibility requirements, lenders typically evaluate the following factors:

Condominium Association Financials: Lenders assess the financial stability and viability of the condominium association by reviewing financial statements, reserve funds, and annual budget. The association should demonstrate adequate reserves and a financially healthy operation.

Commercial Space Limitations: FNMA and FHLMC have limitations on the amount of commercial space allowed within a mixed use condominium project. The maximum commercial space allowed is 35% of the building's total square footage, excluding space used for parking. If the project exceeds the maximum allowable commercial space, it may impact eligibility.

Litigation and Insurance: Lenders review whether the condominium project is involved in any pending litigation that could pose financial or safety risks. They also assess the availability and adequacy of hazard and liability insurance coverage for the project.

VA Eligibility: The VA has specific criteria for approving a condominium project for VA financing, including:

VA Approval or Acceptance (Waiver) : VA-approved condominium projects have gone through a review process to ensure they meet VA requirements. Lenders check if the project is already VA-approved or if it meets VA acceptance criteria.

Financial Stability: Lenders evaluate the financial stability and viability of the condominium association to ensure it is adequately managing the project's financial obligations.

FHA Eligibility: For FHA financing, lenders assess the following factors to determine the eligibility of a condominium project:

FHA Approval: FHA-approved condominium projects have gone through an extensive review process to meet FHA guidelines. Lenders check if the project has FHA approval or if it meets FHA acceptance criteria.

Owner-Occupancy Ratio: The FHA requires a minimum of 35 percent of owner-occupied units within the condominium project.

Financial and Legal Compliance: Lenders review the financial stability of condominium associations, including adequate reserves and appropriate budgeting. They also check for any legal issues or pending litigation that may affect the project's eligibility.

Condominium Project Certification: The condominium association may need to complete the FHA Condominium Project Certification process, providing recent detailed information about the project's compliance with FHA requirements to ensure no material changes have occurred since the date the project was last approved by FHA.

USDA Eligibility: USDA financing for condominium projects in rural and suburban areas follows specific guidelines, including:

Property Location: USDA loans are available for properties located in eligible rural areas as defined by the USDA. Lenders check if the condominium project is within the designated rural area.

Income and Occupancy Restrictions: USDA loans have income limits for borrowers and may have restrictions on the rental or leasing of units within the condominium project.

Association Financials: Lenders assess the financial stability of the condominium association and evaluate its ability to properly manage the project's financial obligations.

It's crucial for real estate agents to work closely with lenders who have experience with the specific financing programs and can evaluate the eligibility of a condominium project based on the applicable agency guidelines. Agents should communicate with lenders early in the process to determine the project's eligibility for financing, as it can impact a buyer's ability to secure a loan for the desired condominium unit.

5.3 Evaluating the Financial Stability of the Condominium Association

Real estate agents should understand how lenders evaluate the financial stability of a condominium association and why this evaluation is essential to a borrower's decision to purchase a unit. Here's an explanation of the evaluation process and its significance:

Reviewing Financial Documents: Lenders typically review the financial documents of the condominium association to assess its financial stability. These documents may include:

Budget: Lenders examine the association's budget to ensure it is well-managed and sustainable. They analyze income sources (such as monthly fees from unit owners), expenses (including maintenance, repairs, insurance, and utilities), and reserve funds.

Reserves: Lenders assess the adequacy of the association's reserve funds, which are set aside for major repairs, replacements, and unexpected expenses. Some states now mandate reserve studies to ensure adequacy of reserve funds to meet the HOA future capital expenditure needs. Sufficient reserves indicate that the association can handle future maintenance or repair needs without burdening unit owners with special assessments.

Delinquency Rates: Lenders review the association's delinquency rates to determine the number of unit owners who are behind on their monthly fees. High delinquency rates may suggest financial instability and the potential for increased fees or reduced services. Most conventional and government lenders will not finance loans if more than 15 percent of the unit owners are 60 days or more delinquent on their HOA or Special Assessment Dues.

Analyzing Financial Ratios: Lenders may calculate financial ratios to gauge the association's financial health. Common ratios include:

Reserve Ratio: This ratio compares the association's reserve funds to its overall budget or total expenses. A healthy reserve ratio indicates that the association has sufficient funds to address future maintenance needs. Most conventional and government lenders require an annual reserve contribution equal to at least 10 percent of their annual assessment. Exceptions can be considered if the HOA has a recent reserve study that supports a lower percentage.

Operating Expense Ratio: This ratio compares the association's operating expenses to its total income. A lower ratio suggests better financial management and the ability to cover expenses without relying heavily on monthly fees or special assessments.

The Significance for Borrowers: The financial stability of the condominium association is vital to a borrower's decision to purchase a unit for several reasons:

Maintenance and Repairs: A financially stable association is more likely to have funds available for regular maintenance and repairs. This helps ensure that common areas, amenities, and building systems are properly maintained and are safe and sound, enhancing the overall living experience and property value.

Avoiding Special Assessments: A financially unstable association may resort to special assessments—additional fees charged to unit owners—to cover unexpected or major expenses. These assessments can be burdensome for unit owners and potentially impact their ability to afford mortgage payments.

Long-Term Financial Planning: A financially stable association with adequate reserve funds demonstrates a proactive approach to long-term financial planning. This indicates that the association is prepared to handle future repairs, replacements, or improvements without imposing financial strains on unit owners.

Lender Requirements: Lenders often require the condominium association to meet certain financial stability criteria for loan approval. If the association does not meet these requirements, it may affect a buyer's ability to secure financing for the unit.

Understanding the financial stability of the condominium association allows real estate agents to inform buyers about potential risks and benefits associated with a particular condominium project. By guiding buyers to assess the financial health of the association, agents help ensure that their clients make informed decisions and choose a financially secure community for their condominium purchase.

5.4 Evaluating Master Insurance

As a real estate agent, it is crucial to understand the importance of a condominium homeowners association (HOA) having the following types of master insurance coverage: Hazard, Liability, Fidelity, and Flood . Here's why it's essential for a condominium HOA to have specific insurance policies in place:

Hazard insurance coverage comes in two primary forms: full replacement cost coverage and actual cash value coverage. The difference lies in how the insurance company calculates the reimbursement amount in the event of a covered loss. Hazard Policies should include: Inflation Guard Coverage; Building Ordinance or Law Coverage; and Boiler and Machinery/Equipment Breakdown Coverage, if obtainable in the insurance market available to the HOA.

Full Replacement Cost Coverage: With full replacement cost

coverage, the insurance company will reimburse the insured party for the cost of repairing or replacing damaged property or items with new ones of similar kind and quality, without deducting for depreciation. This means that the insured party will receive funds to cover the actual cost of rebuilding or repairing the property to its original state, even if the property has depreciated in value over time. Full replacement cost coverage provides more comprehensive protection and helps ensure that the insured can fully restore their property without suffering a financial loss.

Actual Cash Value (ACV) Coverage: Actual cash value coverage takes into account depreciation when calculating the reimbursement amount. It considers the current market value of the property or items at the time of the loss, factoring in their age, wear and tear, and any other relevant depreciation factors. The insurance company will reimburse the insured party for the cost of repairing or replacing the damaged property or items minus the depreciation value. As a result, the payout under actual cash value coverage is typically lower than under full replacement cost coverage, as it reflects the diminished value of the property.

The financial impact of depreciation can be significant for the HOA if it has actual cash value coverage rather than full replacement cost coverage. Here's how depreciation can affect the HOA:

Out-of-pocket expenses: If the HOA experiences a covered loss, such as fire or storm damage, and has actual cash value coverage, the insurance reimbursement may not fully cover the cost of rebuilding or repairing the damaged property to its original condition. The HOA may need to use its own funds to make up the difference, resulting in additional financial strain on the association.

Inadequate repairs or replacements: With actual cash value coverage, the reimbursement amount may not be sufficient to replace damaged property or items with new ones of similar kind and quality. The HOA may be forced to make compromises, using less expensive materials or equipment that may not match the original standards. This can impact the overall quality and aesthetics of the condominium, potentially affecting property values and resident satisfaction.

Increased financial burden on unit owners: If the HOA's insurance coverage is inadequate, it may need to levy special assessments on unit owners to cover the shortfall in funds for repairs or replacements. This can place an unexpected financial burden on unit owners, potentially causing dissatisfaction and financial strain within the community. This is a major reason why conventional and government mortgages require Full Replacement Cost Coverage.

Having full replacement cost coverage is generally considered more desirable for the HOA as it provides better protection and minimizes the potential financial impact of depreciation. It ensures that the HOA can restore the property to its original state without incurring significant out-of-pocket expenses or compromising on the quality of repairs or replacements. HOA's with policies that include a "co-insurance" clause are also acceptable as long as the coverage is at least equal to 100% of the replacement cost value of the project improvements.

As a real estate agent, it's important to educate potential buyers and existing owners about the type of hazard insurance coverage the HOA has in place. Buyers should understand the financial implications and risks associated with actual cash value coverage and inquire about the adequacy of the coverage when considering purchasing a condominium unit.

Liability Coverage: Liability insurance protects the HOA and its members in the event of lawsuits or claims resulting from bodily injury or property damage that occurs on the common areas or due to the actions of the HOA itself. Without liability coverage, the HOA and its members could be personally liable for substantial financial damages, legal fees, and settlements. It provides a crucial layer of protection for both the association and individual unit owners. Under the "Severability of Interest Provision" Each insured party on the master liability policy is treated as if it is covered by its own liability insurance policy.

Fidelity Coverage: Fidelity insurance, also known as employee dishonesty coverage, protects the HOA against losses caused by fraudulent acts committed by employees or board members. This coverage is essential as it helps mitigate the risk of financial mismanagement, embezzlement, or other dishonest activities that could harm the association's financial health and the trust of its members. This coverage is required for conventional and government mortgage financing in attached projects with 21 or more units.

Flood Insurance (Special Flood Hazard Area): If a condominium is located in a Special Flood Hazard Area, Zone "A" or "V" designated by the Federal Emergency Management Agency (FEMA), it is crucial for the HOA to have flood insurance. Standard hazard insurance policies typically exclude coverage for flood damage. Flood insurance ensures that the association and its members are protected against losses resulting from floods, which can be particularly devastating and costly.

By having these insurance policies in place, the condominium HOA can provide a sense of security and peace of mind to unit owners. As a real estate agent, it's important to communicate the significance of these insurance coverages to potential buyers and existing owners. Buyers need to understand the level of protection available to them and the potential financial risks they may face without proper insurance coverage. Existing owners should be aware of the HOA's commitment to risk management and protecting the collective interests of the community.

Additionally, lenders often require proof of these insurance policies to approve mortgage financing for potential buyers. Without the necessary insurance coverage, it can be challenging for buyers to secure financing, limiting the pool of eligible buyers and potentially affecting property values within the condominium.

By emphasizing the importance of these insurance policies, real estate agents can help educate buyers about the role of HOA insurance in protecting their investment and maintaining the financial stability of the condominium community.

5.5 Working with Appraisers and Inspectors in Condominium Transactions

Real estate agents should understand the roles of appraisers and inspectors in condominium transactions and how their roles differ from single-family transactions. Here's an explanation:

Appraisers: Appraisers play an important role in determining the value of a property. In condominium transactions, their role is similar to that in single-family transactions, but there are some notable differences:

Unit Valuation: Appraisers assess the value of individual

condominium units based on factors such as location, size, layout, condition, and comparable sales within the same condominium project or similar projects in the area.

Common Area Evaluation: Unlike single-family transactions, appraisers in condominium transactions also evaluate the value and condition of the common areas, amenities, and shared facilities. This includes assessing the quality, maintenance, and appeal of the building's exterior, hallways, elevators, and other shared spaces.

Market Analysis: Appraisers consider market conditions and trends specific to condominiums in the local area when determining the property's value. They take into account factors such as supply and demand, recent sales data, and the desirability of the condominium project within the market.

Inspectors: Inspectors play a critical role in examining the condition of the property and identifying potential issues or areas that may require attention. In condominium transactions, their role differs slightly from single-family transactions:

Unit Inspection: Inspectors assess the condition of the individual condominium unit, including the interior components, appliances, and systems. They evaluate the electrical, plumbing, heating, and cooling systems, as well as the structural integrity and overall functionality of the unit.

Limited Common Elements: Inspectors may also examine limited common elements associated with the unit, such as balconies, patios, or parking spaces that are exclusive to the unit owner.

Common Areas and Building Systems: While inspectors primarily focus on the individual unit, they may provide observations or general comments on the condition of the common areas and building systems. However, they typically do not conduct a detailed inspection of the entire building or the shared amenities.

Homeowners Association (HOA) Review: Inspectors may review relevant documentation, such as the HOA's rules and regulations, to ensure compliance and inform buyers of any restrictions or obligations associated with the condominium unit.

It's important for real estate agents to guide their clients in selecting qualified inspectors with experience in condominium transactions. Agents should educate buyers on the limitations of inspections in condominium transactions, emphasizing the need to review the HOA's responsibilities for maintenance, repairs, and insurance coverage for shared areas.

By understanding the roles of appraisers and inspectors in condominium transactions and highlighting the specific considerations involved, real estate agents can assist their clients in making informed decisions and ensure a smoother transaction process.

Chapter 6

Special Considerations in Condominium Financing

6.1 Non-Warrantable Condominiums: Understanding the Challenges

Real estate agents should be familiar with the distinction between "warrantable" and "non-warrantable" condominium projects, as it pertains to agency guidelines. Warrantability can significantly impact the financing options available to buyers. Here's an explanation of the difference and the challenges buyers may face with non-warrantable condominium projects:

Warrantable Condominium Projects: Warrantable condominium projects are those that meet the criteria established by mortgage financing agencies such as Fannie Mae and Freddie Mac: Fannie Mae Selling Guide Sec B4-2 and the Freddie Mac Selling Guide Sec 5700. These guidelines provide requirements for project risk analysis including but not limited to:

- Financial stability and viability of the project
- Project condition and marketability
- Master insurance coverage to protect the project from unexpected losses
- Project characteristics and red flags such as litigation

Non-Warrantable Condominium Projects: Non-warrantable condominium projects encompass those projects that do not meet the criteria set by mortgage financing agencies. This category also includes a specific type of condominium known as "condotels." Here are some key characteristics and challenges associated with non-warrantable condominium projects:

Condotels: Condominiums that operate as a combination of a hotel and individually-owned units. The high presence of investor-owned units, transient nature and resort style amenities in condotels makes them non-warrantable.

Unresolved Legal Issues: Condominium projects involved in ongoing litigation or significant legal disputes involving health, safety or habitability issues or litigation that poses financial risk to the HOA are often categorized as non-warrantable until these issues are resolved.

Financial Instability: Projects with inadequate financial reserve, high percentage of dues delinqueny or unstable financial management may be deemed non-warrantable. This can apply to both traditional non-warrantable projects and condotels, where potential financial risks arise from factors such as limited rental income or excessive wear and tear on amenities from transient usage.

Challenges with Non-Warrantable Condominium Projects: Buyers aiming to finance units in non-warrantable condominium projects may encounter several challenges:

Limited Financing Options: Non-warrantable projects may not qualify for conventional financing through mortgage financing agencies like Fannie Mae or Freddie Mac. This limitation reduces the pool of available lenders, potentially resulting in higher interest rates, stricter underwriting requirements, or the need for alternative financing options.

Higher Down Payment Requirements: Lenders may require a higher down payment for non-warrantable condominium projects. Typically, down payment requirements range from 20% to 30% or even higher. This increased down payment serves as a risk mitigation measure for lenders due to the unique characteristics of these properties.

Reduced Resale Potential: The non-warrantable status can impact the resale potential of units within the project. Some buyers may hesitate to purchase units in non-warrantable projects due to limited financing options or concerns about the project's stability, which can affect future marketability.

Limited Refinancing Options: Non-warrantable projects may present challenges when it comes to refinancing existing loans. Lenders may impose stricter requirements or higher interest rates for refinancing non-warrantable units.

Real estate agents should educate their clients about the challenges associated with financing units in non-warrantable condominium projects. It is crucial to work closely with lenders who specialize in financing non-warrantable or condotel units and explore alternative financing options, such as portfolio loans or specialized lenders catering to these unique property types. By guiding buyers through the complexities of non-warrantable financing agents can help their clients make informed decisions and navigate the process more effectively.

6.2 Condominium Conversion Projects: Financing and Marketing Strategies

Financing Strategies: Investors pursuing condominium conversion projects can employ several financing strategies to facilitate their ventures:

Bridge Loans: Bridge loans are short-term financing options that provide funds to purchase and renovate properties for conversion. These loans bridge the gap until the investor secures long-term financing or sells the individual units.

Portfolio Loans: Investors with an existing portfolio of properties may be able to leverage their assets to secure a portfolio loan. This type of financing allows for flexibility in funding the acquisition and renovation of the property, as well as future conversions within the portfolio.

Hard Money Loans: Hard money loans, provided by private lenders or investors, offer quick access to capital but typically come with higher interest rates and shorter terms. These loans can be utilized during the acquisition and renovation phase of the conversion project.

Joint Ventures or Equity Partnerships: Investors may consider partnering with other individuals or companies to pool financial resources and expertise. Joint ventures or equity partnerships can provide additional capital and shared risk in condominium conversion projects.

Market Strategies: Effective market strategies are essential for investors in condominium conversion projects. Real estate agents can assist investors by suggesting the following strategies:

Market Research and Analysis: Thorough market research helps identify areas with high demand for condominiums and potential profitability. Agents can provide insights on demographics, housing trends, and competitive analysis to help investors select the most promising locations for their conversion projects.

Targeted Marketing: Develop targeted marketing strategies to reach potential buyers and create awareness about the upcoming condominium units. This includes utilizing digital marketing, social media platforms, online listings, and engaging with local real estate professionals and networks.

Pre-Sales or Pre-Leasing: Encourage investors to consider pre-selling or pre-leasing units before the conversion project is complete. This strategy can generate cash flow and gauge market demand, providing financial stability during the conversion process.

Pricing and Unit Mix Analysis: Assist investors in determining competitive pricing and appropriate unit mixes based on market demand and comparable sales in the area. Analyzing buyer preferences, such as unit size, amenities, and pricing trends, can help optimize profitability.

Value-Added Features and Amenities: Identify unique selling points and value-added features that differentiate the converted condominium units from existing options in the market. This could include upgraded finishes, energy-efficient features, smart home technology, or desirable amenities.

Collaboration with Local Professionals: Collaborate with local real estate professionals, such as mortgage lenders, appraisers, and property managers, who are familiar with the market and can provide valuable insights and resources for the conversion project.

By assisting investors in selecting appropriate financing strategies and implementing effective market strategies, real estate agents can play a vital role in the success of condominium conversion projects. Agents should stay updated on local market conditions, financing options, and trends in order to provide informed guidance to their investor clients.

6.3 Construction and New Development Financing for Condominiums

Construction Financing: Construction financing refers to the funding obtained by investors or developers to cover the costs associated with constructing a new development. Real estate agents can assist investors by providing information on the following aspects:

Lenders and Loans: Help investors identify lenders experienced in construction financing who offer loans specifically tailored for new development projects. These lenders may include traditional banks, credit unions, or specialized construction lenders.

Loan Types: Familiarize investors with the different types of construction loans available, such as construction-to-permanent loans, which convert to a mortgage after construction is complete, or stand-alone construction loans that require separate permanent financing.

Loan Terms: Explain the loan terms, including interest rates, repayment periods, and draw schedules. It's essential for investors to understand how funds will be disbursed throughout the construction process to cover expenses.

Down Payments and Equity Requirements: Construction loans typically require higher down payments or equity contributions from investors compared to traditional mortgage loans. Agents should advise investors on the financial obligations and potential cash flow considerations involved in construction financing.

Land Acquisition Financing: Land acquisition financing refers to the funds used to purchase land for new development. Agents can provide guidance on the following aspects:

Financing Options: Help investors explore different financing options for land acquisition, such as conventional loans, commercial loans, or private financing from individuals or entities interested in investing in land development.

Loan Considerations: Assist investors in assessing loan terms, interest rates, down payment requirements, and any necessary collateral for land acquisition financing. Additionally, agents can help investors understand the implications of loan terms on their cash flow and overall project feasibility.

Due Diligence: Emphasize the importance of conducting thorough due diligence on the land being acquired, including title searches, environmental assessments, and zoning restrictions. Investors should be aware of any potential issues or constraints that may impact the development plans.

Airspace Rights Financing: Airspace rights refer to the legal rights associated with the vertical space above a property. In some cases, investors may seek financing specifically for airspace rights to develop air rights projects, such as building additional floors or constructing above existing structures. Agents can provide insights on the following:

Legal Considerations: Explain the legal framework surrounding airspace rights and the regulations specific to the jurisdiction where the development is taking place. Investors must comply with local laws and obtain the necessary permits and approvals.

Valuation and Appraisal: Assist investors in understanding how airspace rights are valued and appraised. This process typically involves considering factors such as market demand, zoning regulations, and the potential impact on neighboring properties.

Financing Options: Help investors explore financing options available for airspace rights projects, which may include traditional construction financing, commercial loans, or alternative funding sources that specialize in air rights development.

Real estate agents play a valuable role in educating investors about construction and new development financing, land acquisition financing, and airspace rights considerations. By providing insights into available financing options, loan terms, and legal requirements, agents can guide investors toward informed decisions and help them navigate the complexities of financing new development projects successfully.

6.4 Condominium Projects on Leased Land

Real estate agents should understand the special considerations involved when a condominium project is located on leased land and how this can impact a buyer's decision to purchase a unit. Here's an explanation:

Leasehold Ownership: In a leasehold ownership structure, the condominium project is constructed on land that is owned by another entity or individual, and the developer or condominium association holds a long-term lease for the land. This arrangement differs from traditional fee simple ownership, where the buyer owns both the unit and the land it sits on. Leasehold ownership raises specific considerations for buyers:

Lease Terms and Expiration: Buyers need to review the lease terms, including the length of the lease and the remaining time until its expiration. The lease may have decades remaining, or it could be approaching expiration within a few years.

Lease Renewal and Terms: Buyers should inquire about the options for lease renewal once the initial lease term expires. Understanding the process, potential changes in lease terms, and associated costs is crucial.

Lease Rent and Payment Obligations: Buyers need to be aware of the lease rent or payment obligations associated with the leasehold ownership. This is typically an annual or periodic payment made to the landowner in exchange for the use of the land.

Landlord Restrictions and Control: The landowner may impose certain restrictions or guidelines on the use of the land or the condominium project. Buyers should familiarize themselves with any limitations that could impact their lifestyle or intended use of the unit.

Financing and Mortgage Considerations: Obtaining financing for a unit on leased land may be more challenging compared to fee simple ownership. Fannie Mae and Freddie Mac require the lease to extend for a period of at least 5 years beyond the maturity date of the loan. Lenders may have overlays with more restrictions regarding leasehold properties due to the perceived risk of financing condos on leaseholds.

Impact on Buyer's Decision: The leasehold ownership structure can have several implications for buyers and may impact their decision to purchase a unit:

Affordability: Leasehold units may be more affordable compared to fee simple properties, as the buyer is not purchasing the land itself. This affordability can make the units more attractive to certain buyers who are seeking a lower price point or entry-level options.

Resale Potential: The resale potential of leasehold units may be influenced by factors such as the remaining lease term, lease rent increases over time, and market perceptions of leasehold properties. Buyers should consider the potential challenges they may face when selling the unit in the future.

Financing Challenges: Buyers may encounter difficulties in securing financing for leasehold units. Some lenders may have restrictions or higher requirements for leasehold properties due to the potential risks associated with the lease terms and leasehold ownership structure.

Future Developments: Buyers should consider any future developments or changes to the leased land that may impact their unit or the overall desirability of the condominium project. This includes the possibility of land redevelopment or changes in land use.

Real estate agents should proactively communicate the implications of leasehold ownership to buyers, providing them with a clear understanding of the terms, potential risks, and financing considerations. Agents should also encourage buyers to conduct due diligence, review lease documents, consult with legal professionals if necessary, and assess their long-term plans and financial goals before deciding to purchase a unit on leased land.

6.5 FHA Reverse Purchase Program For Condos

The FHA Reverse Purchase program, also known as the Home Equity Conversion Mortgage for Purchase (HECM for Purchase), is a specialized financing option offered by the Federal Housing Administration (FHA). It enables eligible homeowners, typically those aged 62 and older (including baby boomers), to purchase a new primary residence, such as a condominium, without making monthly mortgage payments.

With the FHA Reverse Purchase program, the buyer provides a substantial down payment, typically from the sale proceeds of their previous home or other financial resources. The remaining portion of the purchase price is financed through an FHA-insured reverse mortgage. The loan balance accumulates over time as deferred interest accrues since the homeowner is not required to make monthly mortgage payments.

The repayment of the reverse mortgage occurs when the homeowner sells the property, moves out, or passes away. At that point, the loan is repaid through the sale proceeds, and any remaining equity belongs to the homeowner or their heirs. The reverse mortgage offers the benefit of allowing baby boomers to purchase a condominium while preserving their financial flexibility by eliminating the obligation of monthly mortgage payments.

As a real estate agent, it's important to understand the FHA Reverse Purchase program and its advantages. By being knowledgeable about this financing option, you can guide baby boomer clients who are interested in purchasing a condo without the burden of monthly mortgage payments.

It's worth noting that the FHA Reverse Purchase program has specific requirements and guidelines. The buyer must meet certain eligibility criteria, such as age and occupancy requirements. Additionally, the condominium being purchased must meet FHA approval guidelines.

Collaborating with mortgage professionals experienced in reverse mortgages and the FHA Reverse Purchase program is essential to ensure a smooth transaction for your clients. These professionals can provide the necessary guidance and support to help baby boomers navigate the process and make informed decisions.

By providing information about the FHA Reverse Purchase program and its benefits, you can assist baby boomer clients in achieving their homeownership goals, offering them a financing solution that allows them to purchase a condo without the need for monthly mortgage payments.

Chapter 7

Market Trends and Strategies

7.1 Identifying and Analyzing Condominium Market Trends

Identifying and analyzing condominium market trends in urban, suburban, rural and resort markets is crucial for real estate agents. By understanding market trends, agents can provide valuable insights to their clients and make informed recommendations. Here's a guide on how to identify and analyze condo market trends:

Monitor Sales Data: Regularly track and analyze sales data specific to the condominium market in your area. This includes monitoring the number of units sold, average sales prices, price per square foot, and the days on market. Look for patterns and changes over time to identify emerging trends.

Stay Informed About New Developments: Keep a close eye on new condominium developments in your target market. Stay updated on upcoming projects, pre-construction sales, and the overall supply of new units entering the market. This information helps assess market saturation, potential competition, and buyer demand.

Study Listing Inventory: Review the inventory of available condominium units in your target market. Analyze factors such as the number of active listings, the ratio of listings to sales, and the average time it takes for units to sell. This data provides insights into market supply and demand dynamics.

Track Pricing Trends: Monitor pricing trends in the condominium market. Look for changes in average sales prices, price appreciation rates, and price differentials between different unit types, locations, or amenities. Analyze how pricing trends are influenced by factors such as market conditions, location desirability, and unit features.

Analyze Market Absorption Rates: Calculate the absorption rate, which is the rate at which available units are sold within a specific time frame. This helps determine the pace of sales and provides insight into market demand. A low absorption rate may indicate slower sales and a buyer's market, while a high absorption rate may suggest a seller's market.

Study Rental Market Data: Analyze rental market data, particularly in popular tourist destinations and resort areas where vacation rentals are prevalent. Assess rental rates, occupancy rates, and trends in rental demand. This information helps gauge investor interest and potential rental income for buyers looking for investment properties.

Keep Up with Local Economic Factors: Understand the local economic factors influencing the urban and resort markets. Stay informed about job growth, tourism trends, infrastructure developments, and any regulatory changes that may impact the demand for condominiums in these areas.

Consult Local Experts: Engage with local real estate professionals, appraisers, and industry experts who specialize in the urban and resort condominium markets. Their insights and expertise can provide valuable perspectives and help validate market trends.

Leverage Technology and Data Tools: Utilize real estate data platforms, market reports, and analytical tools available to real estate professionals. These resources can provide in-depth market data, analytics, and visualizations that aid in identifying and analyzing market trends effectively.

By actively monitoring and analyzing these key factors, real estate agents can develop a comprehensive understanding of condo market trends in urban, suburban, rural and resort areas. This knowledge allows agents to provide valuable guidance to clients, make data-driven decisions, and effectively navigate the dynamic condominium market.

7.2 Pricing Strategies for Selling Condominiums

Comparative Market Analysis (CMA): Perform a comprehensive comparative market analysis to determine the appropriate listing price for the condominium. Evaluate recently sold comparable properties in the area, considering unit size, location, amenities, and condition. Take into account whether the project is warrantable for conventional and government financing or non-warrantable with limited financing options.

Price Positioning: Choose a pricing strategy that positions the condominium competitively in the market. Consider the project's warrantable or non-warrantable status when determining the price range. Warrantable projects may have broader financing options, making them potentially more attractive to buyers and allowing for slightly higher listing prices.

Seller's Objectives: Understand the seller's objectives and motivations. Adapt the pricing strategy to align with their goals, whether it's prioritizing a quick sale or maximizing profit.

Timing Considerations: Assess market conditions, such as supply and demand dynamics, interest rates, and buyer sentiment. Recognize how the project's warrantable or non-warrantable status may influence market dynamics. In a buyer's market, pricing competitively becomes more crucial for non-warrantable projects to attract potential buyers.

Unique Selling Points: Highlight the condominium's unique selling points to justify the pricing strategy. Emphasize desirable features, such as location, amenities, views, and high-quality finishes. Effectively communicating the value proposition can support the chosen listing price.

Price Adjustments: Monitor market activity closely and be ready to make price adjustments if necessary. If the unit receives limited interest or remains on the market for an extended period, consider adjusting the price accordingly.

Market Feedback: Seek feedback from potential buyers, showing agents, and industry professionals regarding the pricing strategy. Use this feedback to fine-tune the pricing strategy and adapt to changing market conditions.

Marketing and Exposure: Develop a comprehensive marketing plan to generate exposure for the condominium. Utilize high-quality visuals, compelling descriptions, virtual tours, and targeted online advertising. Showcase the property's unique features and advantages to attract potential buyers.

Flexibility: Remain flexible throughout the selling process, adjusting the pricing strategy if needed. Be open to consider that market dynamics evolve and buyer preferences change.

Real estate agents should collaborate closely with their clients, leveraging market knowledge, and data to establish an appropriate pricing strategy. By considering these pricing strategies and factoring in the warrantable or non-warrantable status of the project, agents can effectively position the condominium, attract potential buyers, and facilitate a successful sale.

7.3 Marketing Techniques to Attract Condominium Buyers

First-Time Buyers:

Highlight Affordability: Emphasize the affordability and cost benefits of condominium living compared to single-family homes.

Education on Homeownership: Provide resources and educational materials that guide first-time buyers through the purchasing process, including information on financing options and available assistance programs.

Stress Low-Maintenance Lifestyle: Highlight the convenience and reduced maintenance responsibilities associated with condominium living, appealing to busy first-time buyers.

Urban Dwellers:

Emphasize Location Benefits: Showcase the proximity to urban amenities such as restaurants, shopping centers, cultural attractions, and transportation hubs.

Highlight Walkability: Highlight the walkability and access to public transportation options, reflecting the convenience and lifestyle advantages of living in an urban setting.

Urban Lifestyle Promotion: Utilize marketing materials that showcase the vibrant urban lifestyle and the vibrant community atmosphere of the surrounding neighborhood.

Veterans:

Educate on VA Financing: Inform veterans about the benefits of VA loans, which offer favorable terms and low or zero down payment options for eligible veterans.

Highlight Amenities and Security: Emphasize condominium amenities that cater to veterans' needs, such as fitness centers, security features, and convenient access to healthcare facilities and services.

Supportive Community: Highlight the sense of community and social engagement often found in condominium developments, which may be appealing to veterans transitioning from a military environment.

Empty Nesters:

Promote Downsizing Benefits: Emphasize the advantages of downsizing, such as reduced maintenance, enhanced security, and a simplified lifestyle.

Highlight Lifestyle Enhancements: Showcase amenities and features that cater to empty nesters, such as fitness centers, social spaces, and proximity to entertainment and cultural activities.

Stress Lock-and-Leave Convenience: Highlight the freedom

and peace of mind associated with lock-and-leave convenience for empty nesters who may travel frequently or maintain multiple residences.

Vacation Home Buyers:

Emphasize Resort or Beach Proximity: Highlight the condominium's proximity to popular vacation destinations, beaches, or recreational attractions.

Vacation Rental Potential: Showcase the investment potential of the unit as a vacation rental property, highlighting rental income opportunities during periods when the owner is not using the property.

Stress Low-Maintenance Ownership: Highlight the ease of ownership, as vacation home buyers may prefer a property that requires minimal maintenance while still providing a luxurious and comfortable retreat.

Investors:

Highlight Rental Income Potential: Emphasize the investment potential and attractive rental income opportunities associated with the condominium unit.

Market Analysis: Provide investors with in-depth market analysis, rental market trends, and potential return on investment projections for the condominium.

Showcase Property Management Resources: Offer information on property management services or resources to assist investors in managing the property and rental process efficiently.

Impact of Warrantable vs. Non-Warrantable:

Warrantable Projects: Highlight the broader financing options available for warrantable projects, such as conventional and government-backed loans, which can provide buyers with more flexibility and potentially attract a larger pool of buyers.

Non-Warrantable Projects: Emphasize unique features, advantages, or pricing benefits associated with non-warrantable projects. Provide clear explanations to potential buyers about the implications of non-warrantable status, including potential challenges in obtaining financing and any restrictions imposed by lenders.

By tailoring marketing techniques to target specific buyer categories and considering the impact of warrantable vs. non-warrantable status, real estate agents can effectively attract potential condominium buyers and provide them with the necessary information to make informed purchasing decisions.

7.4 Forecasting the Future of Condominium Financing

Forecasting the future of condominium financing considering the limited availability of land in desirable urban and resort areas requires a comprehensive analysis of various factors. While predicting the exact future outcomes is challenging, here are some considerations and approaches to assess the direction of condominium financing:

Market Research and Trends: Monitor current market trends and conduct ongoing research to identify patterns and shifts in the demand for condominiums in your market area. Stay informed about demographic changes, population growth, and economic indicators that impact housing demand.

Policy and Regulation: Keep track of government policies and regulations that affect condominium development. Changes in zoning regulations, incentives for developers, or affordable housing initiatives can influence the availability of financing options and the overall landscape of condominium projects.

Housing Supply and Land Use: Analyze the supply of available land in your target market. Assess whether there are opportunities for redevelopment or repurposing of existing properties. Evaluate the impact of land scarcity on pricing and financing options for condominium projects.

Financing Programs and Incentives: Monitor financing programs and incentives offered by government agencies, lenders, or private organizations to promote affordable housing. Stay updated on programs that provide favorable financing terms, down payment assistance, or tax incentives for developers and buyers of affordable condominiums.

Collaboration with Developers and Lenders: Engage with developers and lenders specializing in condominium projects. Stay connected to industry professionals who are at the forefront of creating innovative financing solutions. Collaborate with them to understand their strategies, challenges, and projections for the future.

Technology and Construction Innovations: Keep an eye on technological advancements and construction innovations that can potentially lower construction costs, increase efficiency, and facilitate the development of condominium projects.

Public-Private Partnerships: Monitor the collaboration between public and private entities in addressing the demand for affordable housing. Explore partnerships between developers, local governments, and non-profit organizations that leverage public resources, land, or funding to support the financing of condominium projects.

Economic Indicators: Assess broader economic indicators, such as interest rates, employment rates, inflation, and economic stability. These factors can influence lending practices, mortgage rates, and the availability of financing options for condominium projects.

It's important to note that forecasting the future of condominium financing is subject to numerous variables and uncertainties. Local market dynamics, economic conditions, and policy changes can significantly impact the outcomes. Real estate agents should regularly update their knowledge and collaborate with industry experts to stay informed about the evolving landscape of condominium financing in their target market.

Chapter 8

Legal Considerations in Condominium Transactions

8.1 Understanding Common Legal Issues in Condominium Transactions

Real estate agents should be aware of common legal issues that can arise in condominium transactions. While it's important to consult with legal professionals for specific guidance, here are some common legal issues that may arise:

Governing Documents: Reviewing the condominium's governing documents, including the declaration, bylaws, and rules and regulations, is essential. Legal issues may arise if these documents contain ambiguous or contradictory provisions or if they conflict with applicable laws.

Title and Ownership Disputes: Disputes related to title and ownership can occur in condominium transactions. These may involve issues such as fraudulent transfers, conflicting claims, undisclosed liens or encumbrances, or disputes over boundaries or common areas.

Financing and Mortgage Issues: Condominium financing can present unique challenges. Issues may include lenders' unique overlay requirements for project eligibility, the financial stability of the condominium association, pending litigation, or restrictions on the percentage of units that can be rented.

Disclosure Requirements: Sellers have disclosure obligations in condominium transactions. Failure to disclose material defects, pending litigation, special assessments, or other significant issues can lead to legal disputes and potential liability.

Association Disputes: Disputes between unit owners and the condominium association can arise over matters such as maintenance responsibilities, use of common areas, enforcement of rules and regulations, assessment disputes, or disagreements regarding association management.

Construction Defects: Defects in the construction or design of the condominium can lead to legal issues. Buyers may seek remedies for construction defects, such as faulty workmanship, water infiltration, structural issues, or inadequate building materials.

Insurance Coverage: Insurance-related issues can arise, including disputes over coverage for property damage, liability claims, or the adequacy of the association's insurance policies. It's important to review insurance coverage, including policies for individual units and the association as a whole.

Environmental and Regulatory Compliance: Compliance with environmental regulations, building codes, zoning ordinances, and other applicable laws is essential. Failure to comply can result in legal consequences, including fines, penalties, or the need for remediation.

Leasehold and Land Use Issues: In some cases, condominiums are located on leased land or have specific land use restrictions.

Legal issues may arise concerning lease terms, renewal options, permissible uses, or conflicts with local zoning regulations.

It's essential for real estate agents to be aware of these common legal issues and guide their clients to seek legal advice when necessary. Agents should recommend that buyers and sellers work closely with experienced real estate attorneys to navigate these potential challenges and ensure a smooth and legally compliant condominium transaction.

8.2 Reviewing Governing Documents

Reviewing governing documents is vital for real estate agents and buyers when considering a condominium purchase. Here's an explanation of the importance of reviewing specific provisions and the impact they can have on a buyer's decision to purchase a unit:

Limitations on Ability to Sell/Right of First Refusal: These provisions may restrict an owner's ability to freely sell their unit. Right of first refusal clauses give the condominium association or other owners the first opportunity to purchase the unit before it can be sold to an outside buyer. Such restrictions can limit marketability and potentially affect a buyer's decision to purchase a unit if they desire the flexibility to sell without restrictions.

Age Restrictions: Some condominiums have age restrictions, typically intended for senior or retirement communities. These provisions specify the minimum age of residents allowed in the complex. Age restrictions can significantly impact a buyer's decision if they do not meet the age criteria or if they prefer a diverse community with residents of various age groups.

Income Restrictions: Certain condominiums impose income

restrictions, limiting residency to individuals or families below a specific income threshold. Buyers who exceed the income limits may be ineligible to purchase or live in these units.

Understanding income restrictions is crucial to ensure a buyer's eligibility and financial compatibility with the community.

Rental Restrictions: Rental restrictions regulate the ability of owners to rent out their units. Some condominiums may have limitations on the duration or frequency of rentals, or they may prohibit rentals altogether. These restrictions can impact a buyer's decision, particularly for those interested in investment properties or for buyers who desire flexibility to rent out their unit in the future.

Amending Project Documents: The process of amending governing documents allows for changes to the rules and regulations that govern the condominium community. Understanding this process is important as amendments can introduce new restrictions, alter existing rules, or impact the overall dynamics of the community. Buyers should be aware of the potential for future changes that may affect their rights and responsibilities as unit owners.

Terminating Legal Status of Project: In some cases, condominium projects may be subject to termination, where the legal status of the project is dissolved. This typically occurs when a supermajority of unit owners agree to terminate the project and sell the property as a whole. Buyers should consider the potential for termination and assess the impact it may have on their long-term ownership and investment.

Unpaid Dues Lien Priority: Unpaid dues or assessments owed by unit owners to the condominium association can result in liens on the property. Understanding the lien priority is essential for buyers, as unpaid dues can lead to legal consequences and potentially affect the marketability of the unit. Buyers should be aware of any outstanding dues and potential financial implications.

Reviewing these governing document provisions helps real estate agents and buyers understand the specific rules, restrictions, and obligations associated with owning a unit in a particular condominium community. It allows buyers to make informed decisions based on their preferences, long-term goals, and ability to comply with the established regulations. Agents should encourage buyers to thoroughly review the governing documents with the guidance of legal professionals to ensure they fully understand the implications before finalizing a purchase.

8.3 Compliance with State and Federal Laws

Compliance with state and federal laws, including the Uniform Condominium Act (UCA), is vital for condominium homeowners associations (HOAs). Real estate agents should understand the importance of HOAs adhering to these laws and how it can impact the warrantability of a condominium project. Here's an explanation:

Legal Compliance and Consumer Protection: State and federal laws provide legal frameworks to protect consumers and ensure fair practices within the condominium industry. Compliance with these laws helps protect the rights of unit owners and promotes transparency, fairness, and accountability within the HOA.

Uniform Condominium Act (UCA): The UCA is a model law that has been adopted, with some variations, by many states to regulate the creation, governance, and operation of condominium associations. The UCA addresses various aspects, including association powers, financial responsibilities, governance procedures, dispute resolution mechanisms, and unit owner rights. Compliance with the UCA ensures that the HOA operates within the legal framework specific to condominiums in that state.

Warrantability and Financing Eligibility: Warrantability refers to a condominium project's eligibility for conventional and government-backed financing, such as loans insured by the Federal Housing Administration (FHA), Department of Veterans Affairs (VA), or purchased by government-sponsored entities like Fannie Mae and Freddie Mac. Lenders often assess the compliance of the condominium project and its HOA with state and federal laws, including the UCA, when determining warrantability.

Lender Requirements: Lenders typically require condominium projects to meet certain criteria to qualify for financing. These criteria often include provisions related to HOA compliance with state and federal laws, financial stability of the association, reserve fund requirements, insurance coverage, and governance practices. Non-compliance or deficiencies in these areas can result in a project being deemed non-warrantable, making it more challenging for buyers to secure financing.

Impact on Marketability and Resale Value: A non-warrantable status due to HOA non-compliance can impact the marketability and resale value of condominium units. Non-warrantable projects may have limited financing options, which can deter potential buyers and reduce demand. This can lead to longer selling periods and potential price reductions, affecting the resale value of units within the project.

Risk Mitigation and Governance Best Practices: Compliance with state and federal laws, including the UCA, helps HOAs mitigate legal risks and protect the interests of unit owners. By following proper governance practices, adhering to financial and reporting requirements, and ensuring compliance with consumer protection laws, HOAs can maintain a favorable reputation and provide a stable environment for unit owners.

Real estate agents should educate buyers about the importance of HOAs complying with state and federal laws, including the UCA. Agents should encourage buyers to review HOA documents, financial statements, meeting minutes, and legal disclosures to assess compliance and potential risks. Working closely with legal professionals, agents can help buyers make informed decisions and understand the implications of HOA compliance on warrantability and the overall value of condominium units.

Chapter 9

Condominium Red Flags

As a real estate agent, understanding potential "red flags" in condominium characteristics is crucial because these factors can significantly impact the warrantability, value, and buyer's decision to purchase units in a condo project. Here are some common red flags that require detailed analysis:

- Projects that Operate as Hotels or Motels
- Projects Subject to Split Ownership Arrangements
- Projects that Contains Multi-Dwelling Units
- Projects that Operate as a Continuing Care Community or Facility
- Non-Incidental Business Arrangements
- Commercial Space and Mixed-Use Allocation
- Recreational Leases and Mandatory Memberships
- Litigation Activity
- Single-Entity Ownership
- Projects in Need of Critical Repairs
- Special Assessments to Fund Critical Repairs
- Inspection Reports that Indicate Critical Repairs are Required

The following is a list of ineligible characteristic, red flags and detailed criteria that Fannie Mae provides in their Selling Guide (Section B4-2) that can contribute to a condominium being deemed non-warrantable:

9.1 Projects that Operate as Hotels or Motels

A project may not be operated or managed as a hotel, motel, or similar commercial entity as evidenced by meeting one or more of the following criteria:

- The HOA is licensed as a hotel, motel, resort, or hospitality entity.
- The HOA or project's legal documents restrict owners' ability to occupy the unit during any part of the year.
- The HOA or project's legal documents require owners to make their unit available for rental pooling (daily or otherwise).
- The HOA or the project's legal documents require unit owners to share profits from the rental of units with the HOA, management company, or resort, or hotel rental company.

In addition to the requirements above, any project with one or more of the following characteristics is ineligible. The project

- is primarily transient in nature;
- offers hotel type services (including those offered by or contracted through the HOA or management company) or characteristics such as registration services, rentals of units on a daily or short-term basis, daily cleaning services, central telephone service, central key systems and restrictions on interior decorating;
- is a conversion of a hotel (or a conversion of a similar type of transient housing) unless the project was a gut

rehabilitation and the resulting condo units no longer have the characteristics of a hotel or similar type of transient housing building;

- is subject to voluntary rental-pooling, revenue, profit or commission sharing agreements with the HOA or management company, or similar agreements that restrict the unit owner's ability to occupy the unit such as blackout dates and occupancy limits to assure an inventory of units for rent on a frequent basis. This may include daily, weekly, monthly or seasonal restrictions;

- is professionally managed by a hotel or resort management company that also facilitates short term rentals for unit owners or projects with management companies that are licensed as a hotel, motel, resort, or hospitality entity;

- is deemed to be ineligible under Freddie Mac's requirements because of condo hotel, resort, transient or short-term rental activity;

- has a legal or common name that contains hotel, motel, or resort, unless the use of hotel, motel, or resort is a reference to a historical use of the building and not reflective of its current use as a residential condo or co-op project;

- is marketed as a hotel, motel, resort or investment opportunity; or

- has obtained a hotel or resort rating for its hotel, motel, or resort operations through hotel ratings providers including, but not limited to, travel agencies, hotel booking websites, and internet search engines.

The following criteria are examples of some common red flags. The lender should perform additional due diligence of the project when any of these characteristics are present:

- 75% or more of the units are owned as investment and second home occupancy - especially when the loan transaction is not a principal residence transaction;
- units that do not contain full-sized kitchen appliances;
- advertisements for daily or short-term rental rates;
- franchise agreements;
- location of the project in a resort area;
- units that are less than 400 square feet;
- amenities that are common in hotels or resorts including spa services, concierge services, rentals of recreational equipment or amenities, childcare services for short-term renters, scheduled social or entertainment activities for short-term renters, airport shuttles, ski lift shuttles or ski lift and trail passes, or other vacation amenities and packages; or
- interior doors that adjoin different units.

9.2 Projects Subject to Split Ownership Arrangements

Projects with covenants, conditions, and restrictions that split ownership of the property or curtail an individual borrower's ability to utilize the property are not eligible for delivery to Fannie Mae. These types of properties include, but are not limited to, the following:

- "common interest" apartments or community apartment projects that are projects or buildings owned by several owners as tenants-in-common or by an association in which individuals have an undivided interest in a residential apartment building and land, and have the right of exclusive occupancy of a specific apartment in the building;
- projects that restrict the owner's ability to occupy the

unit, even if the project is not being operated as a motel or hotel; and

- projects with mandatory rental pooling agreements that require unit owners to either rent their units or give a management firm control over the occupancy of the units.
- These are formal agreements between the developer, association, and/or the individual unit owners that obligate the unit owner to rent the property on a seasonal, monthly, weekly, or daily basis. In many cases, the agreements include blackout dates, continuous occupancy limitations, and other such use restrictions. In return, the unit owner receives a share of the revenue generated from the rental of the unit.

9.3 Projects that Contain Multi-Dwelling Unit Condos

Projects that contain multi-dwelling units are not permitted. These projects allow an owner to hold title to a single legal unit that is subdivided into multiple residential dwellings within the single legal unit, with ownership of the unit evidenced by a single deed and financed by a single mortgage. The sub-divided units are not separate legal units. This restriction applies regardless if the unit owner maintains one or more of the subdivided units as rental units or uses one or more of the subdivided units as accessory or lock-out units.

This provision does not apply to condo projects that allow an individual to buy two or more individual legal units with the intent of structurally and legally combining the units for occupancy as a single-unit dwelling. Mortgages secured by units in these types of projects are eligible for purchase by Fannie Mae provided all of the following requirements are met:

- The unit securing the mortgage represents a single legal unit under a single deed.

- Any construction or renovation to structurally combine units has no material impact on the structural or mechanical integrity of the project's buildings or the subject property unit.

- The individual units must be fully described in the legal description in the mortgage and under a single deed.

- The project's legal documents must have been amended to reclassify the combined units as a single unit in the project.

- All structural renovation to physically combine the units must be completed.

9.4 Projects that Operate as a Continuing Care Community or Facility

Mortgages secured by units in a project that operates, either wholly or partially, as a continuing care community are ineligible for delivery to Fannie Mae. These communities or facilities are residential projects designed to meet specialized health and housing needs and typically require residents to enter into a lifetime contract with the facility to meet all future health, housing, or care needs. These communities may also be known by other names such as life-care facilities.

Projects that make continuing care services available to residents are eligible only if the continuing care facilities or services are not owned or operated by the HOA and residential unit owners are not obligated to purchase or utilize the services through a mandatory membership, contract, or other arrangement.

Continuing care communities are not the same as age-restricted projects. Age-restricted projects that restrict the age of residents but do not require residents to enter into a long-term or lifetime contract for healthcare and housing as the residents age are eligible.

9.5 Non-Incidental Business Arrangements

A condo project is ineligible if the HOA is receiving more than 10% of its budgeted income from non-incidental business arrangements related to the active ownership and/or operation of amenities or services available to unit owners and the general public. This includes, but is not limited to, businesses such as a restaurant or other food- and beverage-related services, health clubs, and spa services.

Non-incidental income from the following sources is permitted provided the income does not exceed 15% of the project's budgeted income:

- income from the use of recreational amenities or services owned by the HOA for the exclusive use by unit owners in the project or leased to another project according to a shared amenities agreement, or
- income from the leasing of units in the project acquired by the HOA through foreclosure.

9.6 Commercial Space and Mixed-Use Allocation

Fannie Mae requires that no more than 35% of a condo project or 35% of the building in which the project is located be commercial space or allocated to mixed-use. This includes commercial space that is above and below grade.

Any commercial space in the project or in the building in which the residential project is located must be compatible with the overall residential nature of the project.

Rental apartments and hotels located within the project must be classified as commercial space even though these may be considered "residential" in nature. Commercial parking facilities can be excluded from the commercial space calculation.

9.7 Recreational Leases and Mandatory Memberships

Loans securing units in condo projects with mandatory memberships that require the HOA members to pay dues to a third-party organization (such as a golf course or other recreational facility) are ineligible for sale to Fannie Mae. The project must be the sole owner of its amenities, though certain exceptions will be allowed when there is a shared amenities agreement between HOAs.

Projects subject to recreational leases are also not eligible. A recreational lease is a long-term lease between the HOA and a third party for access to certain recreational facilities for a specified time period and payment. In these scenarios, the owner of the facilities is often the project's developer or has some financial relationship to the developer and the leases often provide ongoing profit to this party for the duration of the lease. The lease may permit the owner of the facilities to lease the amenities to other parties in addition to the HOA. The HOA may have certain financial, insurance, and other legal obligations under the lease that may be burdensome over time. These leases may or may not provide the project long-term access to the amenities beyond the initial lease term.

When an HOA is part of a master association, the lender is required to evaluate whether the subject property's HOA members are required to participate in a mandatory membership that is managed through the master association. Additionally, the master association may not be subject to recreational leases as described above.

Lenders are encouraged to review the project's legal documents, sales contract, and budget to identify mandatory memberships and recreational leases. Some red flags that a project may require a mandatory membership, or be a party to a recreational lease, is that the amenities may have some of the following characteristics:

- the amenities have a different name from the residential project and may be recognized as a different legal entity from the HOA,
- owners are required to pay large up-front fees to become a member or have access to the amenities,
- owners are required to pay monthly or periodic dues to the entity that owns or operates the amenities (these dues may be paid directly to the owner or operator or they may be paid to the HOA and passed through to the owner or operator),
- the general public may be able to purchase memberships or access passes for the use of the amenities,
- the amenities can be leased or rented to the public for events not hosted by the HOA or its members, or
- HOA members may be subject to block-out dates or other use restrictions.

9.8 Litigation or Pre-litigation Activity

Projects in which the HOA is named as a party to pending litigation, or for which the project sponsor or developer is named as a party to pending litigation that relates to the safety, structural soundness, habitability, or functional use of the project are ineligible for sale to Fannie Mae.

If the lender determines that pending litigation involves minor matters with no impact on the safety, structural soundness, habitability, or functional use of the project, the project is eligible provided the litigation meets one or more of the following:

- non-monetary litigation including, but not limited to neighbor disputes or rights of quiet enjoyment;
- litigation for which the insurance carrier has agreed to provide the defense, and the amount is covered by the HOA's insurance;
- the HOA is the plaintiff in the litigation and upon investigation and analysis the lender has reasonably determined the matter is minor and will result in an insignificant impact to the financial stability of the project;
- the reasonably anticipated or known damages and legal expenses are not expected to exceed 10% of the project's funded reserves;
- the HOA is seeking recovery of funds for issues that have already been remediated, repaired, or replaced and there is no anticipated material adverse impact to the HOA if funds are not recovered;
- litigation concerning localized damage to a unit in the project that does not impact the overall safety, structural soundness, habitability, or functional use of the project; or
- the HOA is named as the plaintiff in a foreclosure action, or as a plaintiff in an action for past due HOA assessments.

Construction defect litigation in which the HOA is the plaintiff is not considered a minor matter unless the HOA is seeking recovery of funds for issues that have already been remediated, repaired, or replaced. In addition, there is no anticipated material adverse impact to the HOA if the funds are not recovered.

9.9 Single-Entity Ownership

A project meets the definition of single-entity ownership when a single entity (the same individual, investor group, partnership, or corporation) owns more than the following total number of units in the project:

- projects with 5 to 20 units - 2 units
- projects with 21 or more units - 20% (FHLMC allows up to 25%)

Units currently subject to any rental or lease arrangement must be included in the calculation. This includes lease arrangements containing provisions for the future purchase of units such as lease-purchase and rent-to-own arrangements.

The following may be excluded from the single-entity ownership calculation:

- units that are owned by the project sponsor or developer and are vacant and being actively marketed for sale; or
- units that are controlled or owned by a non-profit entity for the purpose of providing affordable housing, units held in affordable housing programs (including units subject to non-eviction rent regulation codes), or units held by higher-education institutions for a workforce housing program.

The single-entity ownership requirement may be waived when the transaction is a purchase transaction that will result in a reduction of the single-entity ownership concentration. In such instances, the following requirements must be met:

- units owned by the single entity represent no more than 49% of the units;
- evidence is required that the single entity is marketing units for sale to further reduce single-entity ownership, with the goal of reducing the concentration to 20% or less of the project units;
- the single entity is current on all HOA assessments; and
- there are no pending or active special assessments in the project.

9.10 Projects in Need of Critical Repairs

Projects in need of critical repairs are those needing repairs or replacements that significantly impact the safety, soundness, structural integrity or habitability of the project's building(s), or the financial viability or marketability of the project. Critical repairs include conditions such as:

- material deficiencies, which if left uncorrected, have the potential to result in or contribute to critical element or system failure within one year;
- any mold, water intrusions or potentially damaging leaks to the project's building(s);
- advanced physical deterioration;
- any project that failed to pass state, county, or other jurisdictional mandatory inspections or certifications specific to structural safety, soundness, and habitability; or
- any unfunded repairs costing more than $10,000 per unit

that should be undertaken within the next 12 months (does not include repairs made by the unit owner or repairs funded through a special assessment).

Examples of some items to consider include, but are not limited to, sea walls, elevators, waterproofing, stairwells, balconies, foundation, electrical systems, parking structures or other load-bearing structures.

If damage or deferred maintenance is isolated to one or a few units and does not affect the overall safety, soundness, structural integrity, or habitability of the project, then these requirements do not apply.

Routine repairs are not considered to be critical and include work that is:

- preventative in nature or part of normal capital replacements (for example, focused on keeping the project fully functioning and serviceable); and
- accomplished within the project's normal operating budget or through special assessments that are within guidelines.

A project with an evacuation order due to an unsafe condition, either for a partial or total evacuation of the project's building(s), is ineligible until the unsafe condition has been remediated and the building(s) is deemed safe for occupancy.

9.11 Special Assessments

Special assessments may be current or planned. Lenders must obtain and review the following information for each special assessment to determine if it addresses a critical repair:

- what is the purpose of the special assessment,
- when was the special assessment approved and is it planned

(approved by the unit owners, but not yet initiated by the board) or already being executed,

- what was the original amount of the special assessment and the remaining amount to be collected, and
- When is the expected date the special assessment will be paid in full.

If the special assessment is associated with a critical repair and the issue is not remediated, the project is ineligible.

9.12 Inspection Reports

If a structural and/or mechanical inspection was completed within 3 years of the lender's project review date, the lender must obtain and review the inspection report. The report cannot indicate that any critical repairs are needed, no evacuation orders are in effect, and no regulatory actions are required.

If the inspection report indicates there are unaddressed critical repairs, the project is ineligible until the required repairs have been completed and documented accordingly. The lender must review an engineer's report or substantially similar document to determine if the repairs completed have resolved the safety, soundness, structural integrity, or habitability concerns of the project.

The impact of a condominium being deemed non-warrantable on a buyer's decision to purchase a unit can be substantial. Here are some potential consequences:

a. Limited financing options: Buyers may face difficulty obtaining traditional mortgage financing for a non-warrantable property. This limitation can restrict the pool of potential buyers and make it harder to resell the unit in the future.

b. Higher interest rates: If a buyer does manage to secure financing for a non-warrantable condominium, they may encounter higher interest rates and less favorable loan terms due to increased risk perceived by lenders.

c. Reduced resale value: Non-warrantable properties can have lower resale values due to the limited buyer pool and potential difficulties in securing financing. This can impact a buyer's potential return on investment.

d. Ineligibility for government-backed loans: Non-warrantable condominiums may not be eligible for government-backed loan programs, such as those offered by the Federal Housing Administration (FHA), further limiting financing options for buyers.

It is crucial for buyers to thoroughly assess the warrantability of a condominium before making a purchase decision. Consulting with a real estate professional, reviewing the condominium's financial documents, and working closely with lenders can help buyers understand the potential risks and make informed decisions.

Chapter 10

Condo Confidential: Why Condominium Financing Varies from Lender to Lender

Determining if a condominium project is warrantable for conventional Government-Sponsored Enterprise (GSE) financing (such as Fannie Mae and Freddie Mac) can be a challenge for real estate agents due to limited access to information.

Here's a breakdown of the challenges:

Lack of Public Access to FNMA's Approved Projects Database: Fannie Mae (FNMA) used to have a public database that listed approved condominium projects eligible for financing. This database was a valuable resource for real estate agents as it provided a centralized and easily accessible list of approved projects. However, as of the time of writing your book, FNMA no longer provides public access to this database.

FHLMC's lack of Database: Freddie Mac (FHLMC) also plays a significant role in providing conventional financing for condominium projects. However, at the time of writing your book, FHLMC did not have a database of approved projects, whether public or private. This lack of a comprehensive and transparent database makes it difficult for real estate agents to readily identify eligible condominium projects.

Reliance on Other Sources: Without access to centralized databases, real estate agents must rely on other sources of information to determine if a condominium project is warrantable. This can include contacting individual lenders who may have their own internal lists of approved projects, or seeking guidance from mortgage professionals who are well-versed in the criteria set by FNMA and FHLMC.

Evolving Criteria: GSEs like FNMA and FHLMC may regularly update their criteria for warrantable condominium projects, adding another layer of complexity for real estate agents. Changes in the guidelines can impact a project's eligibility, and without easy access to the latest information, it becomes challenging to stay up-to-date.

Project-Specific Assessments: Since public databases are not available, real estate agents may need to conduct a thorough review of each condominium project's documents and financials to assess its eligibility for GSE financing. This process can be time-consuming and may require collaboration with condominium associations or property management companies.

Regional Variations: Condominium financing eligibility may also vary based on location and regional factors. GSEs may have specific requirements for certain areas, and without a centralized database, real estate agents must navigate through potentially differing guidelines for different regions.

In addition to the challenges related to limited public access to GSE-approved project databases, real estate agents and borrowers must also be aware of the fact that lenders can impose additional, more restrictive rules on top of the agency guidelines set by entities like Fannie Mae and Freddie Mac. These additional rules are commonly referred to as "lender overlays."

Here's why this can be a challenge:

Lack of Transparency: Lender overlays are essentially additional requirements that lenders impose on borrowers beyond what the GSEs specify. These overlays are not required to be disclosed upfront to borrowers or real estate agents. As a result, borrowers may not be aware of these extra criteria until they are already deep into the loan application process, potentially leading to last-minute surprises and complications.

Variation Among Lenders: Lender overlays can vary significantly from one lending institution to another. One lender might have more lenient criteria for condominium project financing, while another might have stricter requirements. This lack of consistency can make it challenging for real estate agents to know with certainty which lenders will be willing to finance a particular condominium project.

Impact on Borrowers' Eligibility: Lender overlays can affect borrowers' eligibility for conventional GSE financing. Even if a condominium project meets the basic criteria set by Fannie Mae or Freddie Mac, the additional requirements imposed by a specific lender might render the borrower ineligible for a loan with that particular institution.

Reduced Pool of Eligible Borrowers: Lender overlays can also lead to a reduced pool of eligible borrowers for certain condominium projects. Some borrowers who would have qualified for financing under GSE guidelines alone may no longer meet the stricter criteria set by certain lenders.

Complexity in Loan Shopping: For real estate agents assisting clients in finding suitable financing options, navigating lender overlays can add complexity to the loan shopping process. Agents may need to work closely with mortgage professionals and borrowers to identify lenders with more flexible criteria for specific condominium projects.

Here are some reasons why lenders may add overlays to their project approval process:

Risk Assessment: Lenders assess the risk associated with financing a particular condo project. They consider factors such as the financial health of the homeowners association (HOA), the occupancy rates, the number of delinquent homeowners, the level of commercial space within the project, and other project-specific characteristics. Lenders may have differing risk tolerances, which can result in more restrictive approval requirements.

Market Conditions: Lenders may tailor their project approval requirements based on market conditions and their own risk management strategies. For example, if they perceive a higher risk of defaults or a decline in property values in a specific area or project type, they may impose stricter guidelines to mitigate potential losses.

Investor Demand: Lenders may have different preferences for the types of loans they want to offer and the investor market they want to serve. Some lenders may prioritize loans that meet specific investor criteria, and as a result, they may impose additional requirements on condo projects to align with those preferences.

Internal Policies and Guidelines: Lenders often establish their own internal policies and guidelines that go beyond the minimum requirements set by FNMA and FHLMC. These additional requirements may be based on their own analysis, historical data, or internal risk management practices.

Secondary Market Considerations: Lenders who plan to sell the loans they originate on the secondary market may need to adhere to the guidelines of the investors or entities purchasing those loans. These secondary market participants may have their own unique requirements for condo project warrantability.

When a lender denies a condo project based on their more restrictive rules, it can result in the borrower incurring various expenses. For instance, the borrower may have already paid for an appraisal, credit report, inspection reports, and condo document fees. These costs can add up to thousands of dollars, all of which become non-recoverable if the loan is ultimately denied. This situation puts an undue financial burden on the borrower and can lead to unexpected expenses.

Furthermore, this process can have negative consequences for the seller as well. When a lender denies a condo project, the property is taken off the market, resulting in lost valuable marketing time. This delay in selling the property can have significant ramifications for the seller, including potential price reductions, missed opportunities, and increased carrying costs.

To address this challenge, real estate agents should encourage borrowers to be proactive in shopping for loans and comparing offers from multiple lenders. They should also work with experienced mortgage professionals who are familiar with different lenders' practices and can help identify suitable financing options for specific projects. Additionally, promoting transparency in lending practices and encouraging lenders to disclose their overlays upfront could help borrowers make more informed decisions when choosing a lender for condominium financing.

Chapter 11

Top Ten Condominium Financing Myths

Accepting condo financing myths, resulting from overlays, as actual agency guidelines can have significant negative consequences for real estate agents, both in terms of missed sales opportunities and risks to their reputation. Here's why:

Missed Sales Opportunities: When real estate agents believe and spread financing myths, they might turn away potential buyers who could have otherwise qualified for a condo loan. For example, if an agent mistakenly believes that all condos are ineligible for FHA loans, they may not show condos to buyers who could have qualified for such financing. This limits the pool of potential buyers and can lead to missed sales opportunities for both the agent and the seller.

Limited Market Knowledge: Relying on financing myths instead of accurate guidelines can result in a limited understanding of the market. Real estate agents need to be well-informed about different financing options available to buyers, especially for condos, which often have specific loan programs tailored to them. Misunderstandings about financing options can make agents less effective at helping their clients find suitable properties and secure financing.

Loss of Credibility: If a real estate agent consistently provides incorrect information about condo financing, they risk losing credibility with both clients and colleagues. Clients depend on their agents to guide them through the complex process of buying a property, including securing financing. If an agent's advice leads to missed opportunities or failed transactions due to financing issues, it can damage their reputation and make it harder for them to attract new clients in the future.

Legal and Ethical Concerns: Providing inaccurate information to clients about financing options could potentially lead to legal and ethical issues. Agents have a duty to act in their clients' best interests, which includes providing accurate and up-to-date information about financing guidelines. Misleading clients, even unintentionally, may lead to disputes or claims of misrepresentation.

Impact on Seller's Interests: For sellers, having an agent who is not well-informed about financing options for condos can be detrimental. It may result in longer marketing periods for the property or accepting offers with less favorable terms because some buyers may not be aware of the available financing options for the condo.

To avoid these problems, real estate agents must stay informed about the current financing guidelines for condos and other types of properties. They should rely on reputable sources and consult with mortgage professionals and lending institutions to get accurate information. Being knowledgeable about financing options and dispelling common myths will not only benefit the agent's business but also provide a better service to their clients, leading to more successful and satisfying transactions.

The following are the top ten condominium financing myths that I encounter on a regular basis by real estate agents who are not familiar actual agency guidelines:

1. Projects with a high percentage of investors are ineligible for conventional (GSE) financing

    FALSE

    As long as the borrower is looking to purchase an owner occupied or second home, investor concentration is not an issue. The only time investor concentration is an issue is when an investor is looking to purchase a unit in a project that already has 50% or more investors.

2. Projects with pending litigation are ineligible for conventional (GSE) financing

    FALSE

    Minor litigation is acceptable. Litigation that poses financial risk to the HOA viability or relates to the safety, structural soundness, habitability, or functional use of the project is ineligible for conventional financing.

3. Projects that allow Daily Rentals are ineligible for conventional (GSE) financing

    FALSE

    Conventional loans do not have a minimum rental period restriction. However, projects that are predominantly transient in nature or operate as a hotel or motel are ineligible.

4. VA and FHA Project Review is a very expensive, time consuming

and complicated process.

FALSE

Neither VA or FHA charge fees for project review. It's absolutely free. Reviews typically take a few weeks to complete once all the required documents have been submitted for review.

5. All Townhome projects are exempt from project review

FALSE

Townhomes are a style of attached housing in horizontal projects which can be legally created as Planned Unit Development (PUD) or condominium. If the townhouse project is created as a condominium then project approval is required for conventional financing.

6. Projects that do not own their own amenities are ineligible for conventional financing

FALSE

Shared amenities are permitted when two or more HOA's share amenities for the exclusive use of the unit owners. The associations are required to have an agreement in place governing the arrangement for shared amenities.

7. VA loans can only be assumed by other veterans

FALSE

Non-veteran buyers that meet the lender's credit and income requirements can assume a VA loan and release the veteran from mortgage loan liability.

8. Condominiums require larger down payments than single family homes

FALSE

Fannie Mae, Freddie Mac down payments for condominiums are the same as single family homes.

9. Condo buyers are required to purchase a HO6 insurance policy in an amount equal to at least 20% of the appraised value.

FALSE

Lenders are prohibited from requiring a borrower to purchase more insurance than what is required. If a HO6 policy is required then the amount of coverage should be determined by the insurance agent and buyer.

10. Projects with income or age restrictions are ineligible for conventional financing

FALSE

Income and age restrictions are allowable resale restrictions for conventional financing.

Conclusion

In this book, real estate agents will gain valuable insights and knowledge essential to mastering the lucrative niche of condominium sales. Throughout its pages, you will discover a comprehensive understanding of the intricacies surrounding condo financing, the impact of various condo characteristics on warrantability, value, and buyer decisions, and how to navigate potential red flags.

By delving into the complexities of condo financing, you will equip yourself with the tools needed to guide buyers through the often confusing landscape of loan options, eligibility requirements, lender "overlays", and agency guidelines. This newfound expertise will enable you to confidently present suitable financing options to clients, ultimately resulting in more closed sales and satisfied buyers.

Furthermore, you will learn to recognize and address red flags associated with condominium characteristics. Armed with this knowledge, you can proactively assist buyers in making informed decisions, offering transparent information that builds trust and confidence in your services.

As you deepen your understanding of the condo market, you will gain a competitive edge in generating more condo sales. By showcasing your expertise, clients will come to rely on you as their go-to agent for condo transactions, leading to increased business opportunities and a growing network of satisfied clientele.

Moreover, this book will be instrumental in helping you build referral opportunities. As you become a trusted expert in the field, satisfied clients will be more inclined to recommend your services to friends, family, and colleagues in search of their own condo investments.

In essence, this book is your gateway to becoming a proficient and sought-after agent in the realm of condominium sales. Through its valuable teachings, you will enhance your ability to navigate complex condo financing, address potential red flags, and provide unparalleled guidance to buyers. Embrace the knowledge within these pages, and witness the transformation of your real estate career as you generate more condo sales, cultivate lasting client relationships, and unlock a wealth of referral opportunities.

Appendix

Form 1076

Condominium Project Questionnaire

ADDENDUM ADDED DECEMBER 2021

Instructions

Lender: Complete the first table below and enter the date on which the form should be returned to you.

Homeowners' Association (HOA) or Management Company: This form has been sent to you on behalf of an individual seeking mortgage financing to purchase or refinance a unit in this project. The mortgage lender needs this information to determine the eligibility of the project for mortgage financing purposes. Complete and return this form by to the lender listed below. Questions about this form should be directed to the lender contact.

Lender Name:	Lender Phone Number:
Contact Name:	Lender Fax Number:
Lender Address:	Lender Email Address:

I. Basic Project Information	
1. Project Legal Name:	
2. Project Physical Address:	
3. HOA Management Address:	
4. HOA Name (if different from Project Legal Name):	
5. HOA Tax ID #:	

6. HOA Management Company Tax ID #:
7. Name of Master or Umbrella Association (if applicable):
8. Does the project contain any of the following? Check all that apply:
a ❑ Hotel/motel/resort activities, mandatory or voluntary rental-pooling arrangements, or other restrictions on the unit owner's ability to occupy the unit
b ❑ Deed or resale restrictions
c ❑ Manufactured homes
d ❑ Mandatory fee-based memberships for use of project amenities or services
e ❑ Non-incidental income from business operations
f ❑ Supportive or continuing care for seniors or for residents with disabilities
Provide additional detail here, if applicable (optional):

II. Project Completion Information		
1. Is the project 100% complete, including all construction or renovation of units, common elements, and shared amenities for all project phases?	Yes	No
If No, complete lines a-f:		
a ❑ Is the project subject to additional phasing or annexation?	❑ Yes	❑ No
b ❑ Is the project legally phased?	❑ Yes	❑ No
c ❑ How many phases have been completed?		
d ❑ How many total phases are legally planned for the project?		
e ❑ How many total units are planned for the project?		
f ❑ Are all planned amenities and common facilities fully complete?	❑ Yes	❑ No
1. Has the developer transferred control of the HOA to the unit owners?	❑ Yes	Date transferred:
	❑ No	Estimated date the transfer will occur:

III. Newly Converted or Rehabilitated Project Information	
1. Is the project a conversion within the past 3 years of an existing structure that was used as an apartment, hotel/resort, retail or professional business, industrial or for other non-residential use?	❑ Yes ❑ No
If Yes, complete lines a-g:	
a In what year was the property built?	
b In what year was the property converted?	
c Was the conversion a full gut rehabilitation of the existing structure(s), including replacement of all major mechanical components?	❑ Yes ❑ No
d Does the report from the licensed engineer indicate that the project is structurally sound, and that the condition and remaining useful life of the project's major components are sufficient?	❑ Yes ❑ No
e Are all repairs affecting safety, soundness, and structural integrity complete?	❑ Yes ❑ No
f Are replacement reserves allocated for all capital improvements?	❑ Yes ❑ No
g Are the project's reserves sufficient to fund the improvements?	❑ Yes ❑ No

IV. Financial Information	
1. How many unit owners are 60 or more days delinquent on common expense assessments?	
2. In the event a lender acquires a unit due to foreclosure or a deed-in-lieu of foreclosure, is the mortgagee responsible for paying delinquent common expense assessments?	❑ Yes ❑ No
If Yes, for how long is the mortgagee responsible for paying common expense assessments? (*Select one*)	❑ 1 to 6 months ❑ 7 to 12 months ❑ More than 12 months
3. Is the HOA involved in any active or pending litigation?	Yes No
If Yes, attach documentation regarding the litigation from the attorney or the HOA. Provide the attorney's name and contact information:	
Attoney Name:	
Attorney Phone Number:	

V. Ownership & Other Information		
1. Complete the following information concerning ownership of units:		
	Entire Project	Subject Legal Phase (in which the unit is located) *If Applicable*
Total number of units		
Total number of units sold and closed		
Total number of units under bona-fide sales contracts		
Total number of units sold and closed or under contract to owner-occupants		
Total number of units sold and closed or under contract to second home owners		
Total number of units sold and closed or under contract to investor owners		
Total number of units being rented by developer, sponsor, or converter		
Total number of units owned by the HOA		

2. Complete the following table if more than one unit is owned by the same individual or entity.

Individual / Entity Name	Developer or Sponsor (Yes or No)	Number of Units Owned	Percentage Owned of Total Project Units	Number Leased at Market Rent	Number Leased under Rent Control
	❑ YES ❑ NO		%		
	❑ YES ❑ NO		%		
	❑ YES ❑ NO		%		
	❑ YES ❑ NO		%		

3. Do the unit owners have sole ownership interest in and the right to use the project amenities and common areas?	❑ YES ❑ NO
If No, explain who has ownership interest in and rights to use the project amenities and common areas:	

4. Are any units or any part of the building used for non-residential or commercial space? If Yes, complete the following table: ❏ YES ❏ NO

Type of Commercial or Non-Residential Use	Name of Owner or Tenant	Number of Units	Square Footage	% Square Footage of Total Project Square Footage
				%
				%
				%
				%

5. What is the total square footage of commercial space in the building that is separate from the residential HOA?
Include above and below grade space used for commercial purposes, such as public parking facilities, retail space, apartments, commercial offices, and so on.

Total square footage of commercial space:

VI. Insurance Information & Financial Controls

1. Are units or common elements located in a flood zone? ❏ YES ❏ NO

If Yes, flood coverage is in force equaling (Select only one option below):

❏ 100% replacement cost

❏ Maximum coverage per condominium available under the National Flood Insurance Program

❏ Some other amount (Enter amount here): $ _____

2. Check all of the following that apply regarding HOA financial accounts:

❏ HOA maintains separate accounts for operating and reserve funds.

❏ Appropriate access controls are in place for each account.

❏ The bank sends copies of monthly bank statements directly to the HOA.

❏ Two members of the HOA Board of Directors are required to sign any check written on the reserve account.

❏ The Management Company maintains separate records and bank accounts for each HOA that uses its services.

❏ The Management Company does not have the authority to draw checks on, or transfer funds from, the reserve account of the HOA.

3. Supply the information requested below. Do NOT enter "contact agent."

Type of Insurance	Carrier/Agent Name	Carrier/Agent Phone Number	Policy Number
Hazard			
Liability			
Fidelity			
Flood			

VII. Contact Information
Name of Preparer:
Title of Preparer:
Preparer's Phone:
Preparer's Email:
Preparer's Company Name:
Preparer's Company Address:
Date Completed:

Condominium Project Questionnaire Addendum

This Addendum is applicable to both condominium and cooperative projects. It must be completed by an authorized representative of the HOA/Cooperative Corporation.

Project Information
Project Name:
Project Address:

Building Safety, Soundness, Structural Integrity, and Habitability	
1. When was the last building inspection by a licensed architect, licensed engineer, or any other building inspector?	
2. Did the last inspection have any findings related to the safety, soundness, structural integrity, or habitability of the project's building(s)?	❑ Yes ❑ No
2a. If Yes, have recommended repairs replacements been completed?	❑ Yes ❑ No
If the repairs/replacements have not been completed:	
2b. What repairs/replacements remain to be completed?	
2c. When will the repairs/replacements be completed?	
Provide a copy of the inspection and HOA or cooperative board meeting minutes to document findings and action plan.	
3. Is the HOA/Cooperative Corporation aware of any deficiencies related to the safety, soundness, structural integrity, or habitability of the project's building(s)?	❑ Yes ❑ No
3a. If Yes, what are the deficiencies?	
3b. Of these deficiencies, what repairs/replacements remain to be completed?	
3c. Of these deficiencies, when will the repairs/ replacements be completed?	

Building Safety, Soundness, Structural Integrity, and Habitability		
4. Are there any outstanding violations of jurisdictional requirements (zoning ordinances, codes, etc.) related to the safety, soundness, structural integrity, or habitability of the project's building(s)?	❑ Yes	❑ No
If Yes, *provide notice from the applicable jurisdictional entity.*		
5. Is it anticipated the project will, in the future, have such violation(s)?	❑ Yes	❑ No
If Yes, *provide details of the applicable jurisdiction's requirement and the project's plan to remediate the violation.*		
6. Does the project have a funding plan for its deferred maintenance components/items to be repaired or replaced?	❑ Yes	❑ No
7. Does the project have a schedule for the deferred maintenance components/items to be repaired or replaced?	❑ Yes	❑ No
If Yes, *provide the schedule.*		
8. Has the HOA/Cooperative Corporation had a reserve study completed on the project within the past 3 years?	❑ Yes	❑ No
9. What is the total of the current reserve account balance(s)?	$	
1. Are there any current special assessments unit owners/ cooperative shareholders are obligated to pay? If Yes:	❑ Yes	❑ No
10a What is the total amount of the special assessment(s)?		
10b What are the terms of the special assessment(s)?		
10c What is the purpose of the special assessment(s)?		

Building Safety, Soundness, Structural Integrity, and Habitability	
11. Are there any planned special assessments that unit owners/ cooperative shareholders will be obligated to pay? If Yes:	❑ Yes ❑ No
11a What will be the total amount of the special assessments?	$
11b What will be the terms of the special assessments?	
11c What will be the purpose of the special assessments?	
12. Has the HOA obtained any loans to finance improvements or deferred maintenance?	❑ Yes ❑ No
12a Amount borrowed?	$
12b Terms of repayment?	
Additional Comments:	

Contact Information	
Name of Preparer:	
Title of Preparer:	
Preparer's Phone:	
Preparer's Email:	
Preparer's Company Name:	
Preparer's Company Address:	
Date Completed:	

Condominium Questionnaire FNMA Form 1076/ FHLMC Form 476 Including Addendum "A" Pertaining to: Building Safety, Soundness, Structural Integrity and Habitability.

Made in the USA
Coppell, TX
16 August 2023